Recent Developments
in the Theory of

INVOLUNTARY
UNEMPLOYMENT

Carl Davidson
Michigan State University

1990

W.E. UPJOHN INSTITUTE for Employment Research
Kalamazoo, Michigan

Library of Congress Cataloging-in-Publication Data

Davidson, Carl.
    Recent developments in the theory of involuntary unemployment /
Carl Davidson.
      p.   cm.
    Includes bibliographical references and index.
    ISBN 0-88099-105-4 (alk. paper). — ISBN 0-88099-106-2 (pbk. :
alk. paper)
      1. Unemployment—Mathematical models   I. Title. II. Title:
Involuntary unemployment.
      HD5707.5.D38 1990
      331.13'7—dc20   90-21175
                                                             CIP

THE INSTITUTE, a nonprofit research organization, was established on July 1, 1945. It is an activity of the W. E. Upjohn Unemployment Trustee Corporation, which was formed in 1932 to administer a fund set aside by the late Dr. W. E. Upjohn for the purpose of carrying on "research into the causes and effects of unemployment and measures for the alleviation of unemployment."

Cover design by J.R. Underhill
Index prepared by Shirley Kessel
Printed in the United States of America

ACKNOWLEDGMENTS

This research was completed with the financial support of the W. E. Upjohn Institute for Employment Research, which I gratefully acknowledge. I also appreciate the helpful comments of the Upjohn Institute staff economists at the seminars that I gave, as well as the comments of my colleagues at Michigan State University who read earlier versions of this manuscript. I am particularly indebted to Paul Chen, Daniel Hamermesh, Harry Holzer, Andrew John, Larry Martin, Steve Matusz, Ed Montgomery, Bob Spiegelman and Steve Woodbury for discussing these issues with me in detail. Finally, I am happy to have this opportunity to thank Steve Woodbury for suggesting and encouraging this project.

THE AUTHOR

Card Davidson received his B.A. degree from Emory University in 1978 and his Ph.D. in Economics from the University of Wisconsin in 1982. He joined the faculty at Michigan State University as an assistant professor in that year, and became an associate professor in 1987. In addition to his work on search-generated unemployment, he has written on the effect of bargaining structure on wages, employment and strike activity, oligopoly theory (including horizontal mergers), the impact of government policies on collusive activity, and tax incidence in the presence of significant market power.

CONTENTS

1
Introduction

The perfectly competitive, frictionless, complete information general equilibrium model has served as the cornerstone to modern economic theory for over 50 years. However, the Walrasian assumption that markets clear necessarily assumes away the possibility of unemployment. This is a particularly disturbing problem for anyone who wishes to consult basic economic theory for guidance. After all, much public debate concerning economic policy revolves around the expected effects of proposed policies on the unemployment rate and the welfare of the unemployed. In light of this and in light of the fact that unemployment exists and persists, it is vitally important for economists to expand their basic paradigm in a manner that would allow for the investigation of issues related to unemployment.

Prior to the 1960s, the amount of work devoted to unemployment was limited. Most studies that focused on unemployment tended to assume that it was due either to a minimum wage, rigid wages, or unions. It is by now well accepted that unions alone cannot cause unemployment as long as a sector of the economy remains nonunionized (see any standard macroeconomic text, such as Parkin 1984). Unions can cause wage differentials across sectors but cannot keep the labor market in nonunionized sectors from clearing. Minimum wages also seem to be an unlikely cause of a significant amount of unemployment, since only a small percentage of the economy's jobs are affected by the minimum wage laws. Moreover, recent empirical evidence provided by Brown, Gilroy, and Kohen (1982) suggests that minimum wages do not contribute significantly to adult unemployment (although they can be viewed as a significant contributor to teenage unemployment). Finally, models with rigid wages are of little value unless they also provide an explanation of the cause of the rigidity; otherwise, it is impossible to predict how various policies will affect unemployment and real wages. Therefore, little, if any, success at understanding the phenomenon of unemployment was achieved prior to 1960.

In contrast, over the past 25 years the causes and consequences of unemployment have been a major focus of much research. Most of the studies have remained in the traditional paradigm, but have extended the basic model by dropping one or more of the assumptions that lead to market clearing. For example, in models with unemployment generated by search, the assumption that unemployed workers and firms with vacancies are instantaneously matched is replaced with the assumption that it takes time and effort for the trading parties to find each other. Other lines of research have introduced unemployment by allowing for incomplete information in the marketplace (the implicit contracts and efficiency wage literatures) or by assuming that quantities adjust faster than prices to clear markets (the fixed price or disequilibrium literature). In each case, however, most of the studies have tended to focus on the technical details and the theoretical aspects of the models and little has been done to make these new theories accessible to the majority of the profession and policymakers. Moreover, only recently have these theories been developed to the point that serious empirical investigations could be undertaken.

The purpose of this monograph is to provide a nontechnical summary of the most prominent theories of unemployment that have emerged since 1960: search, disequilibrium (i.e., fixed price models), implicit contracts, efficiency wage, and insider/outsider models. This is accomplished by reviewing selected articles in each of the areas and distilling their arguments to the bare essentials. In this manner, I am able to focus on the overall purpose of each line of research, its strengths, and its major weaknesses. I have attempted to keep as much of the discussion at as nontechnical a level as is possible by relying heavily on graphs and intuitive arguments, with some occasional elementary calculus. The level of technical difficulty varies with topic. For example, many of the arguments in the implicit contracts chapter are presented graphically. On the other hand, some basic calculus is required in part of the chapter on search theory. By presenting the material in this manner, I hope to make the new theories more accessible to the profession and shorten the time lag that usually exists between the development of a new theory and the empirical work that is necessary to test its implications.

The monograph consists of five chapters in addition to the introduction. Chapter 2 is devoted to the search literature; beginning with Stigler's classic article on the economics of information and proceeding gradually to the general equilibrium search models of Diamond (1981, 1982a, 1982b, 1984a, 1984b). In chapter 3, I turn my attention to the fixed price or disequilibrium literature. Coverage of this topic includes discussion of the work by Barro and Grossman (1971), Malinvaud (1977), and Benassy (1982). Since one of the major insights provided by this literature is that the most effective policy for combating unemployment depends upon which markets are out of equilibrium (in addition to the labor market), I emphasize the relationship between the appropriate policy prescription and the structure of market disequilibrium. Recent work on imperfect competition in a general equilibrium setting and the "coordination failures" that may result are also reviewed in this chapter, with careful attention given to how this work relates to the earlier fixed price models. Chapter 4 is devoted to the literature on implicit contracts. Here, particular emphasis is placed on the difficulties this line of research encountered in attempting to explain the coexistence of wage rigidity and unemployment in a contracting framework. Chapter 5 covers the newest theories of unemployment—the efficiency wage and insider/outsider theories of unemployment. Finally, in chapter 6, a summary of the important insights provided by each theory is complemented by a discussion of the important questions that remain to be addressed.

Before beginning, a brief word about the theories I have and have not chosen to review in the monograph is in order. Most notably absent is the "rational expectations" approach to macroeconomics developed by Lucas, Sargent and Wallace, among others. This line of research differs from those reviewed here in one fundamentally important aspect: it rejects the Keynesian approach to macroeconomics and unemployment while the theories that I have chosen to survey can be viewed as attempts to provide a solid microeconomic foundation for the Keynesian model. This important distinction is explained in the following passage from Diamond (1984b).

> To contrast with equilibrium models, I will start with a
> strawman Keynesian model. Prices and wages are given.
> Resources are allocated on the basis of these prices and a

rationing mechanism. Prices and wages then adjust in response to the presence of rationing and past inflation rates. We can see that this model is not micro based: transactions are occurring at prices that neither clear the market nor come from an explicit micro source that might generate trade at nonclearing prices; furthermore, price adjustment is not related to any explicit consideration of self-interested price setting or price negotiations. Nevertheless, a model based on this approach can be developed to give a reasonably good fit to aggregate time series data. In addition this is a simple framework that can be readily used for macro problems and policies.

There are at least two possible reasons for constructing micro-based models as an alternative to this approach. One is a belief that the Keynesian model is basically wrong. The second is a belief that the model can be improved by reconstruction from a micro foundation. The former is represented by the rational-expectations equilibrium approach to business cycles; the latter by my search-equilibrium approach [and the other literatures surveyed here]. There is a problem of vocabulary here. The [search] model I presented in the first lecture has rational expectations, is an equilibrium model, and can be viewed as an alternative to the Keynesian model; yet it is not the type usually referred to as a rational-expectations equilibrium model. Such a description is usually applied to the models pioneered by Lucas, which I refer to as the classical market approach.

The classical market approach says that the economy may have the appearance of slow, nonclearing price and wage movements, but that actually markets clear. The combination of small price and wage movements is due to large intertemporal substitutabilities and misperceptions of relevant relative prices. Such misperceptions are necessarily present when markets are incomplete; that is, observed nominal prices are not adequate guides to intertemporal relative prices. Note that market clearance and market nonclearance are mutually exclusive views of the world.

Diamond then goes on to argue (convincingly) that his search framework provides models that are better able to explain micro data (such as price dispersion) and fit macro data than the rational-expectations counterparts. In addition, he argues that the insights generated by his model are much more robust with respect to changes in the underlying assumptions. Although I believe that similar arguments hold for the other models of unemployment surveyed here, I will not press this issue. Instead, I will simply note that with its market-clearing framework, the rational-expectations approach only provides an explanation for fluctuations in employment and output or, at best, voluntary unemployment. In this monograph, I restrict attention to theories of involuntary unemployment, that is, theories that are consistent with or provide a rationale for Keynesian macroeconomics.

2
Search Theory

In the standard Walrasian general equilibrium model, trade is coordinated by a fictitious auctioneer who instantaneously matches buyers and sellers. In addition, since prices adjust to equate supply and demand, all desired transactions take place at a single price or wage, the one that clears the market. Therefore, price or wage offers are never rejected by potential trading parties. In the search literature, unemployment is generated by dropping one (or sometimes both) of these assumptions. Search models assume that it takes time and effort for trading parties to find each other. In addition, firms are allowed to offer different equilibrium wages so that workers sometimes find it optimal to reject a wage offer they consider too low. Workers who cannot find a firm with a vacancy or workers who cannot find a firm offering a sufficiently high wage remain unemployed. In such a setting, determinants of the unemployment rate include the search technology (the process that matches workers and firms), the cost of search, and the wage-offer distribution.

Although search models have provided insights into a wide variety of labor-oriented issues, in this chapter I focus solely on their potential value for understanding unemployment. In addition, rather than attempt to provide a complete survey, my goal is to offer a critical overview of the literature's historical development with an emphasis on the usefulness of the models for policy analysis. In section B, I review papers that adopt a "partial-partial" equilibrium approach. This phrase, coined by Rothschild (1973), indicates that these models focus on only one side of one market, i.e., the supply side of the labor market.[1] Most of the studies in this category begin by assuming that firms offer different wages and that unemployed workers search by contacting firms until they find a wage offer they consider acceptable. The major result supplied by this literature is a fairly complete characterization of the optimal search strategy for an unemployed worker in a variety of environments.

To adequately investigate both the effects of policies aimed at reducing unemployment and the hardship associated with joblessness, a full equilibrium model is essential. The partial-partial equilibrium approach tells us how policies affect the behavior of unemployed workers by altering their incentives to accept or reject wage offers. However, the fact that the firm's problem is never explicitly modeled (and therefore no explanation of the origin of the wage-offer distribution is provided) severely limits the number and type of questions that can be addressed in this framework. Two different approaches have emerged to close the model in a manner that would permit one to address policy issues: the "reservation wage" and "trade friction" approaches.[2]

Section C is devoted to an analysis of the reservation wage approach. The studies that fit into this category generally build on models introduced in the partial-partial equilibrium literature by endogenizing the wage-offer distribution. This allows for an investigation of the influence of worker search behavior on firm behavior. Moreover, it allows for a study of the types of incentives created by various policies and their impact on labor demand. Unfortunately, most of the results from this literature must be characterized as negative (or, at best, ambiguous) and, at the end of the section, it is argued that further work along these lines is not likely to be fruitful.

The newest and, in my opinion, most promising line of research is reviewed in section D. This literature focuses on the difficulty that firms with vacancies and unemployed workers face in trying to find each other. Both sides of the market are modeled as active searchers attempting to locate a trading party in a friction-filled world. Such models are commonly referred to as "trade friction models." One of the most important insights provided by this line of research is that the individual's search decision is riddled with externalities. This result implies that all equilibria are (generally) suboptimal and gives rise to arguments for corrective policies. Moreover, it has been demonstrated that when search is required to find employment, there is a natural tendency towards multiple equilibria. This result further suggests that an active government might improve the performance of the economy by guiding it to the "best" equilibrium.

An additional insight provided by the trade friction literature concerns the inherent social value of a job. Most economists would agree that, if we ignore equity considerations, the social value of a job is fully captured by the value of the stream of output it produces. This is certainly true of employment in frictionless Walrasian general equilibrium models. However, when frictional unemployment is present and workers are finitely lived, it has been shown that each job carries with it a surplus value above and beyond the value of the output it produces. The intuition for this result runs along the following lines. When search is required to find employment, a worker currently holding a job is more likely to be employed in the future than his or her jobless counterparts. Moreover, new generations entering the labor force must incur at least a brief spell of unemployment as they search for their first jobs. Therefore, since the current cohort of workers includes both employed and unemployed workers, while future generations begin their careers unemployed, the share of tomorrow's economic pie enjoyed by members of today's generation increases with current employment. In addition to implying that jobs are more valuable than the output they produce, this result also implies that generations will differ in their assessments of labor market policies. This has important implications for the optimal labor market policies in the presence of search-generated unemployment.

Before beginning, a few words about the approach taken in this survey are in order. First, as a prelude to the review, I begin in section A by providing a simple dynamic model of the labor market designed to show how flows into and out of employment influence the equilibrium level of unemployment. This allows me to refer to the model in future sections in order to emphasize which aspects of unemployment can and cannot be explained by the different models. Second, many of the studies reviewed, especially those in sections B and C, focused on the implications of search in product markets. However, since I am concerned solely with the implications in terms of unemployment, I will take the liberty of presenting the results as they apply to the labor market.

A. Labor Market Dynamics

The unemployment rate changes over time for a variety of reasons. Unemployed workers find jobs, employed workers quit to seek a better job, firms lay off part of their labor force, and so on. To examine the effects of policies aimed at reducing unemployment, we need to understand how these flows into and out of employment are determined and how they interact to produce an equilibrium level of unemployment. In this section I provide a simple dynamic model of the labor market that allows me to address the second issue.[3] In the subsequent sections, models of worker and firm search aimed at explaining the different components of job turnover are reviewed.

To describe the evolution of the labor market over time, the following notation is introduced (t denotes the time period):

N_t = the number of labor force participants

U_t = the number of unemployed workers

μ_t = the unemployment rate

NE_t = the number of new entrants into the labor force

R_t = the total number of retirements

UR_t = the number of unemployed workers who choose to retire

Q_t = the number of workers who quit to seek a new job

J_t = the number of unemployed workers who find a job

S_t = the number of unemployed workers unwillingly separated from their job (i.e., laid off or discharged).

My goal is to explain how the equilibrium unemployment rate, $\mu = \dfrac{U}{N}$, is linked to movements into and out of employment. To begin with, it can be shown that, if the time between periods is small, the rate of growth of μ is (approximately) equal to the rate of growth of unemployment less the rate of growth of the labor force. That is,

$$(1) \qquad \frac{\Delta\mu}{\mu} = \frac{\Delta U}{U} - \frac{\Delta N}{N}.$$

Equilibrium occurs when the unemployment rate remains constant over time (i.e., $\Delta\mu = 0$); or, from (1), when the level of unemployment grows at the same rate as the labor force. This fact is used below to solve for μ^*, the equilibrium rate of unemployment.

First, I describe how the size of the labor force and the level of unemployment are determined. The number of labor force participants changes over time as new workers enter and others retire. Assuming that the decision to enter the labor force is made at the beginning of each period while the decision to retire is made as the period ends, it follows that

(2) $N_t = N_{t-1} + NE_t - R_{t-1}$.

Now consider unemployment. Workers leave unemployment if they find a job or retire; they enter the unemployment pool if they are fired or quit (layoffs are included in the first category). New entrants also contribute to unemployment as they join the labor force jobless and immediately begin searching for employment. The dynamics of U_t are described in equation (3) under the assumption that job terminations occur at the end of the period.

(3) $U_t = U_{t-1} + NE_t + Q_{t-1} + S_{t-1} - UR_{t-1} - J_{t-1}$.

It is important to note that workers who quit or lose their jobs are not immediately rehired by some other firm (therefore, Q excludes those workers who quit in order to accept another job immediately). This is due to the assumption that it takes time and effort to find a suitable job. Without this assumption, equilibrium would always be characterized by full employment.

The number of quits, separations, retirements, new entrants, and new jobs depends on the current composition of the labor force. At each point in time, I assume that a constant fraction of all labor force participants chooses to retire. This fraction, which is assumed to be independent of the worker's employment status, is denoted by r. Therefore, $R_{t-1} = rN_{t-1}$ and $UR_{t-1} = rU_{t-1}$. In addition, the current labor force gives birth to new workers so that the number of new entrants may be represented as a fraction of the current labor force. The birth rate is represented by b. Consequently, $NE_t = bN_{t-1}$. From (2), it follows that the labor force grows at a rate of $b - r$:

(4) $\dfrac{\Delta N_t}{N_{t-1}} = \%$ change in $N = b - r$.

A similar analysis can be used to describe the rate of growth of unemployment. Quits and involuntary separations are written as fractions of employment with q and s denoting the proportion of workers quitting or losing their jobs, respectively. In other words, $Q_{t-1} = q[N_{t-1} - U_{t-1}]$ and $S_{t-1} = s[N_{t-1} - U_{t-1}]$. Finally, e denotes the proportion of unemployed workers who find employment in any given period so that $J_{t-1} = eU_{t-1}$. Substituting these values into (3) and solving yields the rate of growth of unemployment:

(5) $\dfrac{\Delta U_t}{U_{t-1}} = \dfrac{b + q + s}{\mu_{t-1}} - (r + e + s + q).$

We are now in a position to solve for the equilibrium rate of unemployment. This is accomplished by substituting (4) and (5) into (1), setting $\Delta\mu$ equal to zero, and solving for μ. We obtain

(6) $\mu^* = \dfrac{b + q + s}{b + q + s + e}.$

μ^* is inversely related to the job finding rate (e) and positively related to the quit, job separation, and birth rates (q, s, and b). Intuitively, an increase in any of the flow rates *into* unemployment results in a higher equilibrium unemployment rate, while an increase in the flow rate *out* of unemployment lowers the natural rate. Therefore, insights into the impact of policies on unemployment can be gained by examining how the policies influence these flows into and out of employment.

From the worker's point of view, the flow rates represent hazard rates, i.e., the per period probability of changing employment status. Central to the search theoretic framework is the assumption that these values lie strictly between zero and one. This implies that there is randomness involved in movements from one employment state to another. Workers may attempt to reduce the randomness by altering search behavior, but cannot eliminate it entirely. Most of search theory can be viewed as an attempt to explain how search behavior and the market interact to determine these hazard rates.

Finally, to close this subsection, I would like to offer a few words about the empirical relevance of the different hazard rates. Several facts about job turnover are well known. First, over 60 percent of the workers who quit move immediately into another job; that is, few quits are followed by nontrivial spells of unemployment.[4] Historically, only 10–15 percent of the newly unemployed choose to leave their job.[5] Second, most workers who are unemployed have held jobs previously.[6] These workers either lost their jobs through layoffs or job terminations or are reentering the labor market after a spell of nonparticipation. This class of workers accounts for well over 60 percent of unemployment.[7] These two facts imply that s, the separation rate, is the most important factor in explaining transitions into unemployment. Third, unemployment spells occur frequently, but most are of short duration. Although the average duration varies across the business cycle, it is usually the case that about half of the unemployed have been without a job for fewer than six weeks. Very few searchers remain unemployed more than 27 weeks.[8] This suggests that for the typical searcher s and e are not insignificant. Finally, quits are countercyclical while separations vary procyclically. This fact implies that layoffs and job terminations are the most important determinant of the cyclical component of unemployment.[9] Moreover, combining these facts leads to the conclusion that the quit and birth rates are far less important than s and e in explaining the unemployment process.

B. The Partial-Partial Approach

(i) Optimal Search When Unemployed

The earliest search models focused on the manner in which unemployed workers find employment; or, in terms of the model above, the determinants of e, the job finding rate. This literature originated as a response to the following observations. The Walrasian model predicts that, in equilibrium, there should be a unique wage associated with each type of employment opportunity. Casual observation suggests that in reality this is not the case. In fact, we often observe workers with similar jobs, skills, and work histories earning different wages. Moreover, these wage differences persist over time, suggesting that wage dispersion is an equilibrium phenomenon.

The first two papers that attempted to explain and deal with these facts were George Stigler's classic 1961 piece "The Economics of Information" and its 1962 companion paper "Information in the Labor Market." Although other issues were addressed, the primary contribution of these papers was to raise the question of how an unemployed worker *ought* to go about finding a job in such an uncertain environment. To be more precise, suppose the worker knows the distribution of wage offers but does not know which firm is offering the highest wage.[10] Information may be gathered by contacting individual firms and obtaining wage offers, and then the worker may accept the best offer received. The question is: what is the best strategy to use when searching across firms? Or, what is the best way to search for the highest wage?

Stigler postulated that the optimal search strategy would be to visit a *predetermined* number of firms, N, and then accept the best offer. N would be determined by comparing the expected gain from an additional search with the cost. If the expected gain dominated the cost, N would be increased. If, on the other hand, the marginal cost outweighed the expected gain, N would be deemed too large. The optimal number of firms to sample would therefore be the number that equates the expected gain from searching once more with the marginal cost of search. Assuming that the marginal cost of search is nondecreasing, this value is unique, since additional search yields diminishing returns (the probability of finding a wage above your current best offer falls as more firms are contacted).

Stigler's two papers garnered a great deal of attention. In fact, most (if not all) of the work surveyed in this chapter can be viewed as an extension of his work. However, his conjecture about the optimal search strategy was, for the most part, incorrect. The basic problem is its *nonsequential* nature: the worker decides upon N *before* actually searching, contacts all N firms, and then accepts the best offer. This strategy might make sense if it takes a significant amount of time for the firm to decide how much compensation to offer the worker. In such a setting, N can be interpreted as the number of applications filed by the worker. If, on the other hand, the firm can respond quickly, Stigler's rule can lead to behavior that is clearly suboptimal. For example, suppose the first firm contacted is offering the highest wage in the distribution. Since the worker cannot gain anything from searching further, he or she should stop searching and accept the job. However, even in this situation, the nonsequential search rule dictates that the worker must continue searching until all N firms have been contacted. Clearly, this is not optimal behavior, as a cost is incurred with each unnecessary search.

The problem with nonsequential search was pointed out by J.J. McCall in his 1965 paper "The Economics of Information and Optimal Stopping Rules." In that paper, McCall demonstrated that the optimal search rule involves a sequential process in which the worker decides whether or not to continue searching after obtaining each wage offer. The rule used is very appealing and can be explained in the following manner. Suppose the worker has contacted a firm and has the opportunity to accept a job paying a wage w. If the worker continues to search, there is a potential benefit in that he or she might find a firm offering a higher wage. In deciding whether to stop searching, this expected gain must be compared to the cost of contacting an additional firm.

Let $G(w)$ denote the expected gain and $c(w)$, the cost of search. These values are depicted in figure 2.1. $G(w)$ is downward sloping since a worker holding a relatively high current offer knows that the probability additional search will yield a better offer is small and, even if such an offer is obtained, the increase in lifetime income is likely to be small. Turn next to the cost of search. If we let x denote unemployment compensation and v represent the value of leisure, then the cost of search is equal to $w - (x + v)$ since, by rejecting the offer, the worker chooses to remain idle and collect $x + v$ rather than earn w during the period. It follows that, since the cost of search is increasing in w, there is a unique wage, w^*, that equates the gain from additional search and its cost. This wage, called the worker's reservation wage, allows for a simple characterization of the optimal search rule: search until finding a firm offering compensation at or above the reservation wage.[11] This rule is optimal in the sense that it maximizes the expected value of future income.[12]

Figure 2.1

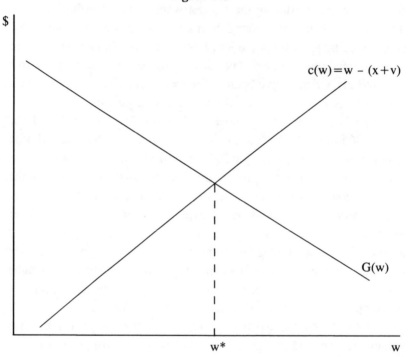

With the optimal search rule in hand, we are now in a position to describe how the job finding rate is determined in the simple wage search models. The job finding rate (e) is equal to the probability that the worker accepts a job in any given period; that is, the probability that the worker receives an offer above the reservation wage. Formally, let λ denote the per period probability of receiving an offer and let $F(w)$ represent the cumulative distribution function of the wage offers. Then it follows that $e = \lambda[1 - F(w^*)]$. Since the reservation wage depends on the form of the wage-offer distribution, the value of leisure, and unemployment insurance, these factors also determine e.

Finally, it is also worth noting that changes in the expected duration of unemployment are linked to changes in the reservation wage. This follows from the fact that an increase in w^* implies that the worker is more likely to reject any randomly chosen wage offer. This increases the expected length of time it takes for the worker to find (what is considered) suitable employment.

Returning now to figure 2.1, it is possible to investigate the effects of various labor market policies on the search behavior of the unemployed. For example, an increase in unemployment compensation (x) lowers the cost of search by reducing the cost of rejecting an offer. This, in turn, increases the worker's reservation wage and leads to a longer expected duration of unemployment. Intuitively, reducing the cost of search allows the worker to hold out for a better job. However, since the wage offers are unchanged (an issue to be discussed below), it obviously takes the worker more time to find acceptable employment. In terms of the model presented in section A, an increase in unemployment compensation lowers e and, if no other rates change, increases μ^*.

Another recently suggested policy provides a bonus payment to workers who find employment within a specified length of time (as in Woodbury and Spiegelman 1987). This policy makes any offer appear more attractive, since acceptance allows the worker to collect the bonus immediately. Therefore, the bonus increases the level of foregone income associated with a rejection, which causes the cost of additional search to rise. This, in turn, lowers the reservation wage and shortens the length of time needed to find employment. The full implications of these and additional policies are discussed at length in section E below.

Before moving on, it should be pointed out that implicit in the model presented above is an assumption that the worker cannot influence the rate at which offers are received. In reality, of course, the worker can increase this rate by searching more intensely.[13] There are a number of ways to extend the analysis to allow search effort to be chosen optimally. The method used by Benhabib and Bull (1983) is especially appealing for our purposes since it combines the approaches developed by Stigler and McCall discussed above.[14] Define the length of a period to be equal to the amount of time it takes for a firm to respond to the worker's inquiry concerning possible employment. Benhabib and Bull allow the worker to choose the number of firms to contact in a given period and then, at the end of the period, when all offers have been made, the worker decides whether to accept the best offer or keep searching. Marginal analysis is used to find the optimal number of contacts and the reservation wage is derived using a method analogous to McCall's. One of their findings is that the worker will typically choose to apply for employment at more than one firm, but that the number of contacts made will be less than the number dictated by Stigler's non-sequential search rule. In addition, in a similar setting, Morgan (1983) shows that an increase in unemployment compensation decreases the number of firms contacted, thereby reinforcing the policy's negative effect on the worker's reservation wage.

(ii) Optimal Search When Employed

Quits can be analyzed in a search theoretic framework by extending the analysis above to allow for on-the-job search. This has been done by Burdett (1978) and Benhabib and Bull (1983). Both papers follow a similar approach in that they allow for different search intensities on and off the job, and both papers obtain similar results. While unemployed, the worker searches with an intensity that equates the expected gain from additional effort with its marginal cost. The worker accepts the first job offering a wage above the return earned while idle, i.e., the value of leisure plus unemployment compensation. Once employed, additional search may be warranted if the current job does not pay enough. However, since the return to additional search is decreasing in the current wage, the worker's optimal search effort declines as better jobs are found. Finally, if the worker secures employment at a high enough wage, search ends altogether. Therefore, with on-the-job search there are two reservation wages, $\underline{w}^*$ and $\bar{w}^*$. If unemployed, the worker accepts the first wage offer above $\underline{w}^*$, but continues to search if the wage is below $\bar{w}^*$. While searching, each job offer paying more than the worker's current job is accepted. Should a job offering compensation above $\bar{w}^*$ be found, the job is accepted and no further search occurs. Quits occur whenever an employed worker receives a better offer.

An alternative model of quits has been provided by Jovanovic (1979, 1984).[15] In these papers, Jovanovic assumes that the worker's productivity is unknown at the time of employment. Over time, both the firm and worker gain information about this unknown value and, hence, the value of the job. If the information is favorable, the wage adjusts accordingly and the worker remains employed. If, on the other hand, the information implies that the worker is not very productive on the current job, the worker's wage falls and quitting may be optimal. Search on the job is allowed so that the worker may be able to move immediately to another job. However, if no current offer is sufficiently high, the worker may find it optimal to quit and begin searching full time for a better job (depending on the market opportunities perceived). Note that the Burdett and the Benhabib and Bull models can only explain movements from job to job, while the Jovanovic assumption that the value of a job is revealed over time provides an explanation of quits followed by a spell of unemployment. This is a nontrivial distinction since, as discussed in section A, quits resulting in a movement from job to job do not contribute to unemployment.

(iii) Other Insights

The partial-partial model of labor supply has been used by a number of authors to address a host of issues. For example, it can be shown that the standard sequential search model predicts that the reservation wage should fall over time for workers who are liquidity-constrained or nearing retirement (see note 11). If such is the case, then as these workers remain unemployed their probability of leaving unemployment rises (since they become more willing to accept a job). This feature is known as "positive duration dependence." For workers with a constant reservation wage, the theory predicts no duration dependence; that is, the probability of leaving unemployment should be independent of the length of time the worker has been without a job. Therefore, the theory provides predictions concerning the time path of hazard rates.

Unfortunately, the empirical evidence on this issue is mixed (see Salant 1977, Heckman and Borjas 1980, and Heckman and Singer 1982 for details).

The simple search model also provides explanations for positively sloped wage/tenure profiles. In the Burdett model of on-the-job search, workers who have been in the labor force for a longer period of time are more likely to be earning a higher wage simply because they have had a longer time to search. The higher wage need not reflect greater productivity. This prediction also falls out of the Jovanovic model, since workers remaining on the job for a long period of time do so because they have proven to be highly productive and have therefore been adequately rewarded. In this case, the higher wage does reflect greater productivity to some degree.

A number of other predictions can be derived from the simple version of the partial-partial search model, or some variant of it, and a great deal of effort has been expended to test these predictions. Many of these predictions concern changes in search behavior either over the life cycle or over the spell of unemployment. For this reason, these results allow us to infer the distributive effects of various policies. Although such effects are clearly important, they are beyond the scope of this review. Moreover, these results have been reviewed elsewhere. Interested readers are referred to the excellent survey by Mortensen (1986).

(iv) Criticisms

The papers reviewed above are said to adopt a partial-partial equilibrium approach because they focus solely on the supply side of the labor market. No attempt is made to analyze the firm's problem, and therefore they cannot provide an explanation of job turnover induced by employer behavior (layoffs and other forms of job termination). Even more seriously, since the behavior of firms is not modeled, it is impossible to investigate how workers' search behavior and government policies influence the employment practices of profit-maximizing firms. For example, if an increase in unemployment compensation increases the reservation wage of all workers, how will this affect the wages firms are willing to offer? It is conceivable that firms, finding it difficult to hire workers at their old wage, will increase their wage offers enough that the expected duration of unemployment will actually be lower once a new equilibrium is established. It is therefore dangerous to attempt to draw policy conclusions from such a limited modeling framework. In fact, results from models in which firm behavior is explicitly analyzed suggest that conclusions drawn from partial-partial equilibrium models may be extremely misleading.

C. The Reservation Wage Approach

(i) The Basic Problem

The value of the papers reviewed in section B lies in their characterization of the optimal search strategy for workers in an uncertain environment. This provides us with a model of the supply side of the labor market and allows us to investigate how policies influence the search behavior of workers. To complete the model, a demand side must be added. This can be accomplished in a number of ways, but two particular methods have dominated the literature. These two approaches share some similarities, but focus on different aspects of the unemployment problem. To be more precise, to become employed a worker must find a firm offering a job at a sufficiently high wage. Therefore, a worker may remain unemployed for two reasons: either no offers are obtained or no acceptable offers are obtained. The trade friction approach (discussed in section D) focuses on the former problem and assumes that all equally productive workers earn the same wage rate. In such a setting, the driving force behind unemployment is the rate at which firms with vacancies and unemployed workers establish contact. On the other hand, the reservation wage approach focuses on the problem of finding a firm willing to offer (what the worker considers) adequate compensation. In this case, only wage offers above the worker's reservation wage are accepted and therefore, for rejections to occur, it must be the case that firms offer different equilibrium wages. Unemployment is then determined by the distribution of reservation wages and its relationship to the distribution of wage offers.

The reservation wage approach grew out of early criticisms of the partial-partial equilibrium models. As noted above, there are reasons to be skeptical of policy conclusions drawn from models that do not account for the behavior of agents on both sides of the market. This skepticism led to attempts to close the original search models in a logically consistent manner. Intuitively, one might have thought that this would be a simple task. After all, it seems obvious that if search costs vary across workers, an equilibrium could be established in which some firms offer low wages and attract only a few workers while other firms pay higher wages and attract a greater supply of labor. The high-wage firms would sell more output but would also be burdened by a larger wage bill so that, in equilibrium, their profits would exactly match those of low-wage firms. Unfortunately, the first attempt to prove the existence of such an equilibrium produced a devastating result: in a model with wage-setting, profit-maximizing firms and workers who search optimally while facing non-zero search costs, the unique equilibrium is characterized by all firms offering the same wage. In addition, the equilibrium wage is identical to what would be offered by a monopsonist (see, e.g., Diamond 1971).

This result, that optimal search by labor eliminates the need to search, created a dilemma. How could one use search theory to model the supply side of the labor market when optimal behavior on the demand side implies no need to search? In other words, although the original search models of Stigler and McCall seemed to provide an intuitively appealing framework in which to analyze unemployment and its consequences, this result implied that when the full labor market equilibrium is derived, all wage dispersion and search disappears.[16] By the same token, although search models were initially developed in an attempt to explain equilibrium price and wage dispersion, optimal search actually eliminates all incentives to offer different wages. Therefore, imperfect information and unequal search costs across workers cannot be the sole sources of the wage dispersion that leads to search.

An enormous literature developed during the 1970s and early 1980s in an attempt to find a way out of the problem created by this negative result. Most studies attempted to provide a model of search in which equilibrium price and/or wage dispersion could be supported. Below I outline the proof that wage dispersion cannot persist in the environment described above in an attempt to shed some light on the types of forces that can result in a nondegenerate equilibrium wage distribution.

Consider a market consisting of a large number of profit-maximizing, wage-setting firms. Suppose that workers search for employment sequentially and that all workers face non-zero (but not necessarily equal) search costs. Let k denote the lowest of these search costs. Finally, suppose that the market is currently characterized by wage dispersion. Can this situation persist? In other words, can this be an equilibrium? To see that the answer is no, consider the plight of the firm offering the highest wage ($\hat{w}$) and, therefore, the best job. What would happen if this firm changed its wage offer? There would be two effects. First, this might change the number of workers who accept the firm's offer. Second, such a change might cause those workers who choose to accept the job to work a different number of hours, i.e., there might be an individual labor supply response. By definition, this second response will increase profits only if the firm moves its wage closer to the monopsony wage. The first effect will be non-negative if the firm increases its wage and non-positive if the firm lowers its wage. Therefore, we can immediately conclude that if the firm's wage is below the monopsony wage, it can increase its profits by increasing its wage offer.

What about the more interesting case in which the high-wage firm is currently offering a wage above the monopsony wage? A lower wage would imply greater profit *if* the firm could guarantee that it would not lose any workers due to the wage cut. Suppose that the firm lowers its wage offer by $kr/2$, with r denoting the discount, i.e., interest, rate. Would any worker who would have accepted an offer at the higher wage ($\hat{w}$) now find it optimal to reject the lower wage and continue searching? The answer is no. Searching once more costs the worker at least k and yields a benefit of at most $kr/2$ per period for the rest of the worker's life (this benefit is only realized if the worker is lucky enough to find another firm offering $\hat{w}$ in the very next period). An infinite stream of $kr/2$ beginning next period has a present discounted value of $k/2$. Therefore, the expected benefit to continued search must be smaller than its cost, which implies that any worker who would have accepted the higher offer would be also willing to accept the lower offer. It follows that, in this case, the firm gains by cutting its wage offer.

We have now shown that the firm offering the highest wage can always increase its profits by changing its wage offer unless the firm is offering the monopsony wage (w^m). However, if the firm is paying w^m, then other firms offering lower wages could increase their profits by increasing their offers towards w^m. Therefore, either the high-wage firm faces an incentive to alter its offer or low-wage firms benefit from raising their offers. Since this implies that at least one firm can increase its profits, our original wage distribution cannot represent a labor market equilibrium. Moreover, it should be clear that the *only* labor market equilibrium is characterized by all firms offering the monopsony wage.

These arguments can be summarized as follows. Search costs, no matter how small, provide the firm with a small amount of monopsonistic power. This power lies in the fact that small wage cuts will not cause the firm to lose workers or job applicants. The firm will not want to reduce its wage offer only when it is paying the monopsony wage. It follows that firms will only offer different wages if they disagree as to the value of the monopsony wage. This would occur, for example, if they possessed different technologies but would never occur if the firms were identical.

(ii) Solutions

There are two ways to alter the analysis above in a manner that allows for a nondegenerate equilibrium wage-offer distribution. The simplest way is to assume that labor productivity (and thus, the monopsony wage) varies across firms. This approach was originally suggested by Reinganum (1979) and has been used by Albrecht and Axell (1984) to develop a general equilibrium model with search-generated unemployment. A brief description of the Axell and Albrecht model and their results shows both the importance of using a fully consistent equilibrium model for policy analysis and the problems associated with closing the model in this manner.

To keep the model as simple as possible, Albrecht and Axell consider an economy with only one factor (labor) and one produced good. Perfect competition (with complete information) is assumed to prevail in the product market while in the labor market workers must search for jobs knowing only the distribution of wage offers. To generate an equilibrium with wage dispersion, they introduce heterogeneity on both sides of the labor market. On the supply side, they assume that there are two types of workers, distinguished by the value they place on leisure. On the demand side, productivity is assumed to vary across firms. A job is created each time a worker accepts an offer and the job dissolves when the worker retires (or, in Albrecht and Axell's terminology, when the worker dies). Equilibrium is achieved when workers search optimally, given the wage distribution and firms offer profit-maximizing wages, given the distribution of reservation wages. Once equilibrium is characterized, the effects of an increase in unemployment compensation are examined.

With only two types of workers, there can be at most two equilibrium wages. To see this, let w_1 denote the reservation wage of the workers who place a relatively low value on leisure and let w_h represent the reservation wage of the remaining workers. While searching, the unemployed consume leisure and therefore, those who value leisure greatly are less anxious to find a job. Consequently, $w_h > w_1$. Now, consider the problem of a typical profit-maximizing firm. Does it ever make sense to offer any wage other than w_h or w_1? Certainly not. The firm can guarantee that each job offer it makes will be accepted by offering a wage at or above w_h. Therefore, there is no reason to offer a wage above w_h. What about wages below w_h but greater than or equal to w_1? Such an offer would be accepted by all job applicants who place a low value on leisure and rejected by all other workers. Since this is true for all wages between w_h and w_1, a profit-maximizing firm would never offer a wage between the two values. Finally, if the firm offers a wage below w_1, no worker would accept and the firm would earn no profit. Therefore, in equilibrium, only two wages are offered. The low wage is equal to the reservation wage of the impatient searchers and the high wage is equal to the reservation wage of those workers who place a relatively high value on leisure. Impatient workers accept the first job offer they receive and the remaining workers search until finding a firm paying the high wage. The total number of unemployed workers is therefore equal to the number of individuals who place a relatively large value on leisure and cannot find a high-wage firm.

To complete the description of equilibrium, we need to explain how active firms decide which wage to offer. Let q_i denote the constant marginal product of a worker at firm i and let P denote the price of the produced good. Some firms, those with q_i less than $\frac{w_1}{P}$, will choose not to produce. This follows from the fact that for these firms the marginal revenue product of labor falls short of the cost of hiring cheap labor. All other firms will produce and earn non-negative profit. Firms with a relatively high value for q_i can afford to pay high wages since their workers are very productive. Firms with a relatively low value of q_i (but a value above $\frac{w_1}{P}$) prefer to offer the low wage and hire only impatient searchers. There is a unique productivity value, q^*, such that a firm with $q_i = q^*$ is indifferent between offering the high and low wages. Therefore, all firms with values of q_i between $\frac{w_1}{P}$ and q^* offer w_1 and all firms with q_i greater than q^* pay w_h. Finally, let γ denote the proportion of active firms paying the high wage. As γ rises, it becomes easier for patient workers to find a high-wage firm and, thus, unemployment falls.

We can now describe how changes in unemployment compensation affect the equilibrium unemployment rate. We noted in section B that an increase in unemployment compensation causes the reservation wages of all workers to rise. Since patient workers spend more time searching, the impact on their reservation wage (w_h) is greater. As w_1 and w_h increase, some firms leave the market (since they can no longer afford to pay even the low wage) and some firms originally offering the high wage switch and offer the low wage (since the gap between the high and low wages has widened). In other words, the number of active firms and the number of high-wage firms both decrease. Unemployment is linked to γ, the proportion of firms offering the high wage, and since this value is equal to the ratio of high-wage firms to active firms, unemployment may rise or fall. In general, the effect on unemployment depends on the distribution of the productivity parameter (q_i) across firms.[17]

This result illustrates two points. First, conclusions drawn from a partial-partial equilibrium analysis may be misleading. Even though an increase in unemployment compensation does result in higher reservation wages, when firms are allowed to react to this change they may do so in a manner that actually reduces the unemployment rate. Second, in order to generate an equilibrium characterized by wage dispersion, it is necessary to introduce heterogeneity on both sides of the labor market. While this may seem appealing in that it probably mimics reality, it results in at least two problems. To begin with, the underlying heterogeneity may be difficult to characterize. After all, for any given level of unemployment compensation there will almost assuredly be more than one distribution of q_i consistent with the observed wage distribution. Subsequent changes in unemployment insurance will nonetheless have very different effects on the unemployment rate (depending on the true q_i distribution). Thus, although it is clearly important, the distribution of q_i cannot be inferred from observable data such as wages. The key data, the values of q_i, seem impossible to specify. Second, even if we ignore this problem, introducing heterogeneity on both sides of the market produces a complex model that yields few (if any) unambiguous predictions. This follows from the fact that the equilibrium wage distribution, unemployment rate, and comparative static properties will depend on the *ad hoc* specification of the underlying distributions describing the degree of heterogeneity in the market. In other words, in order to explain one stylized fact (wage dispersion), a fact that is probably not a major contributor to unemployment, the reservation wage approach must sacrifice tractability and analytic simplicity. In the next section I argue that the trade friction approach, a framework that ignores wage dispersion and focuses instead on the difficulty searchers face in finding *any* employment opportunity, is much more likely to be able to provide insights into the problems associated with search-generated unemployment.

An alternative model of equilibrium wage dispersion can be found in Burdett and Judd (1983). On the surface, their model appears to be a significant improvement over the Reinganum and Albrecht/Axell approach, since it produces wage dispersion without introducing heterogeneity. The fact that they are indeed able to explain wage dispersion in a model with identical rational agents on both sides of the market provides us with some comfort in that it confirms our earlier intuition that incomplete information can be an important source for sustained price disparity. Unfortunately, as I will argue below, their approach can only yield limited insights concerning policy effectiveness for exactly the same reason that the Albrecht and Axell paper fails.

Burdett and Judd generate wage dispersion by changing the description of the search process. They analyze two models. In the first, workers file applications with firms at the beginning of the period and then receive offers as the period ends (as in Benhabib and Bull 1983). When facing such lags in the hiring process it is optimal for workers to search non-sequentially. Assuming that they do so, searchers are likely to observe more than one wage offer before making their decision. Let π_i denote the probability that a worker receives i offers at the end of the period. Then Burdett and Judd show that there are two types of equilibria that may occur, depending on the distribution of π_i. If $\pi_1 = 1$, then all firms pay the monopsony wage. In this case, even though workers may apply for more than one job, they always receive exactly one offer per period. Since this yields a model virtually equivalent to the sequential search model, it is not surprising that wage dispersion cannot exist. The second case is more interesting. When π_1 lies strictly between zero and one, so that with some positive probability the firm has complete monopsony power over a worker, there may be a dispersed distribution of wage offers in equilibrium. Not surprisingly, the form of the wage distribution is tied to the number of applications filed (through the distribution of π_i), which in turn depends on the common search cost. If search costs are relatively low, then Burdett and Judd show that the monopsony wage equilibrium and two dispersed wage equilibria exist. On the other hand, if search costs are relatively high, only the monopsony wage equilibrium will appear. Wage dispersion becomes possible (when search costs are low) because with positive probability some workers receive more than one offer, so that, unlike the case in which workers search sequentially, a small decrease in the wage offered may cause a firm to lose some potential new hires.

A second form of the search process, labeled "noisy search," is also considered. With noisy search each worker pays a fixed fee (c) at the beginning of the period and then receives a random number of job offers. The purchase of a newspaper that includes advertisements for a variety of products would be an example of noisy search in the product market. Making use of a private employment agency might qualify as an example in the labor market. In this case the π_i described above would still be interpreted as the probability of receiving i offers but these values would no longer be tied to c (they are exogenous). This opens up the possibility of a third type of equilibrium—one in which $\pi_1 = 0$ and all firms pay the perfectly competitive wage. Intuitively, since $\pi_1 = 0$, no firm possesses monopsony power over any worker, in that the firm is assured that any worker it tries to hire has at least one other offer in hand. This leads to competition across firms that drives the wage down to the competitive level. Combining this case with the two described above completely characterizes equilibrium with noisy search for any fixed distribution of π_i and for any c.

The Burdett and Judd analysis demonstrates that price and/or wage dispersion can arise in a very simple setting—one with identical, rational, payoff-maximizing, uninformed agents. Unfortunately, their framework does not lend itself to policy analysis any more than does the Albrecht/Axell approach. Consider first the case of nonsequential search. If the cost of search is large, then the unique equilibrium displays no wage dispersion and our original problem of optimal search destroying incentives to search arises again. If the cost of search is low, there are multiple dispersed wage equilibria. In this case, even if one could decide which equilibrium to work with, it would, in general, be difficult to tease out unambiguous comparative static predictions. It is highly likely that the results will depend on the form of the wage distribution, just as in the Albrecht/Axell paper. Policy analysis would be even more difficult in the presence of noisy search since the distribution of π_i is determined outside the model. Different assumptions concerning this distribution will lead to different equilibrium wage distributions and, of course, different comparative static results. In both cases, of course, there is still the problem of finding a way to infer the key parameters (the distribution of π_i) from the available data.

At this point, it is useful to step back and summarize the advantages and disadvantages of this approach. On the positive side, the reservation wage approach has clarified the types of forces that can explain persistent wage dispersion. Although it took nearly a decade, it has confirmed our intuition that wage dispersion may be the result of incomplete information about the availability and quality of job offers. It has also shown us that the amount of information collected in the search process is an important determinant of the amount of wage dispersion that can be supported in equilibrium. The fact that firms need not offer identical wages in equilibrium is also appealing in that it is consistent with observation and allows for the possibility that workers may choose to reject some job offers.

On the negative side, to generate an equilibrium in which equally productive workers earn different wages, we are required to work with models that are hard to characterize, in that the key parameters are often unobservable, and models that seldom yield clear-cut, intuitive predictions. In other words, we must sacrifice simplicity and tractability. If one truly believes that wage disparity and job rejections play important roles in the unemployment process, then the sacrifice is probably worth making. If not, then the unemployment problem stems more from the difficulty of finding a vacant job opportunity rather than finding one offering adequate compensation. If the latter is true, then it is sufficient to work with models with a single wage rate and focus on the determinants of the rate at which firms with vacancies and unemployed workers are matched. This is the approach adopted in the trade friction literature.

How important are job rejections for explaining unemployment? For some subgroups this is clearly an important factor. Feldstein and Poterba (1984) have shown that the reservation wages of displaced workers are generally at or above the wage they earned on their last job. For this reason, displaced workers often have difficulty finding new jobs. In fact, in one survey, the median *reemployed* displaced worker was unemployed for 40 weeks (Hamermesh 1987)! These workers generally find employment only when their reservation wages fall significantly. On average, the real wage earned on their new job is approximately 10 percent below the level earned on their previous job (Hamermesh 1987). A similar problem exists for unemployed black youth (Holzer 1986). One possible explanation for this group is that they misperceive the distribution of wage offers available to them. When they first enter the labor market, their reservation wages are unjustifiably high and they reject too many reasonable job offers. After awhile, they learn about the true distribution, adjust their expectations downward, and accept employment. For other workers, the role of job rejections is less clear cut. For example, Holzer (1987, 1988) reports that unemployed teenagers accept approximately 80 percent of the job offers they receive. What does this imply about adult rejection rates? On the one hand, the ratio of the expected wage to the value of leisure is probably lower for teenagers than for prime-age wage earners and, thus, the rejection rate of adults may be even lower. On the other hand, prime-age adults face smaller separation rates, implying a longer expected duration of employment. This suggests that adults may be more reluctant to accept what they consider a low-paying job. In a 1976 survey of 3,200 unemployed workers, Rosenfeld (1977) found evidence supporting the view that, in fact, adults reject fewer offers than teenagers. Only 10 percent of the workers searching for employment rejected an offer.

D. The Trade Friction Approach

(i) Externalities

The foundations of the trade friction framework can be found in a series of papers by Peter Diamond (1981, 1982a, 1982b, 1984a, 1984b), Dale Mortensen (1982a, 1982b), and Christopher Pissarides (1984a, 1984b). In each of these papers, jobs are viewed as the outcome of a process in which idle factors of production must actively search each other out before production can take place. An underlying "matching technology" (also referred to as the "search technology") describes how search effort on both sides of the market translates into employment. This technology may be viewed as a production function with jobless workers, their search effort, vacancies, and the search effort of firms as the inputs and jobs as the output. Government policies influence the unemployment rate either by altering the flow of inputs into this production process or by changing the form of the matching technology.

Although they differ in specifics, the basic structure of all trade friction models is as follows. In each period, idle factors of production search for employment opportunities. Once a job is located, the firm and worker bargain over the wage rate and then, assuming they can reach agreement, production begins. The duration of a job is assumed stochastic, dissolving with an exogenously given probability in each period. Each time a worker and firm are separated, they each reenter the labor market and begin searching again. Equilibrium occurs when workers choose a level of search effort that maximizes expected lifetime utility, firms choose a level of search effort that maximizes expected profit, and the flows into and out of employment are equal. While flows into employment are governed by the matching technology, search effort, and the level of unemployment, the rate of job separation is usually assumed to be exogenous.[18]

Unemployment occurs whenever a jobless worker fails to find an employment opportunity or fails to reach an agreement with the firm he or she is bargaining with. Unlike the reservation wage approach, the trade friction approach assumes that all equally productive workers earn the same wage, i.e., the bargaining process leads to the same wage for all equally productive workers. The single wage assumption does not necessarily imply that all job offers will be accepted. If the value of the match is stochastic, it is possible that even when potential trading parties meet, it may be optimal to continue searching for a better match. However, in contrast to reservation wage models, job rejection is not the primary reason for unemployment. Instead, in trade friction models, the primary focus is on the determination of the rate at which workers and firms meet. Even when some job offers are rejected, it is the search technology that drives the model. By ignoring wage dispersion and focusing on the search technology, it is possible to build simple, intuitively appealing models that make policy analysis fairly straightforward.

Before digging into the specifics of the various models, I would like to begin by providing an overview of an important insight supplied by the trade friction literature. The result that I wish to focus on is that, in the presence of trading friction, equilibrium will almost certainly be suboptimal. This result is somewhat surprising since, in general, when agents possess no market power, competitive economies operate efficiently. However, this is not the case in the presence of search-generated unemployment. This result follows from the fact that individual search decisions are riddled with externalities. Two types of externalities are most prevalent.[19] The first, labeled "congestion externalities," arise because increased search activity on one side of the market affects the probabilities of employment on both sides. For example, increased search effort by an unemployed worker lowers the probability that other workers will find employment (a negative externality), while making it easier for firms to fill vacancies (a positive externality). Even if a change in one agent's search activity has a small effect on the employment probabilities of other agents, the number of agents so affected will be large, so that the aggregate effect may be nontrivial. These congestion externalities lead to an inefficient level of search activity; but, since both positive and negative externalities are involved, there may be too much or too little search.

I refer to the second type of externality as an "income externality" for lack of a better term. In deciding how hard to search, each worker takes into account the fact that expected lifetime income increases each time a job offer is accepted (relative to what it would be if the offer were rejected). However, the worker ignores the fact that acceptance of the offer also increases the firm's profits by allowing the firm to fill a vacancy. Likewise, when a firm settles on its recruiting intensity, it ignores the positive effect it will bestow on its workers when hiring them. Since these positive external effects are ignored when search decisions are made, income externalities lead to too little search.

If congestion externalities result in too little search, then the two external effects reinforce each other. This leads to a level of search activity below the social optimum. What does this imply about the efficiency of unemployment? The answer to this question depends on the nature of the search process. If, for example, workers and firms search at a constant intensity with a reservation wage in mind, then workers will be too willing to accept a job (their reservation wages will be too low) and firms will be too willing to employ workers (their reservation wages will be too high). Or, in terms of the model presented in section A, the job finding rate (e) will be too high. It follows that, in this case, unemployment will be too low and welfare would be enhanced if all workers raised their reservation wages and all firms lowered theirs by a small amount. This result is reversed, however, if search intensity is a choice variable. When workers or firms can vary their search intensities, too little search activity implies that more effort should be invested in the search process. Since increased effort increases the probability of successful search, too little search translates into an unemployment rate that is too high.

When congestion externalities imply too much search, the two external forces work in opposite directions and the implications for unemployment are ambiguous. In a recent paper, Davidson, Martin, and Matusz (1987a) developed a general equilibrium model with search-generated unemployment and isolated the congestion and income externalities in an effort to understand the conditions under which this would occur. To provide some insight into exactly how these models work and to provide a basis for the policy discussion to follow, I now turn to a brief description of our model and results.[20]

The Davidson, Martin, and Matusz model consists of two sectors and two factors of production. For expositional purposes, the factors will be referred to as capital and labor and the sectors will be referred to as manufacturing and agriculture. Factor markets in the agricultural sector are frictionless and competitive, so that employment is always readily available and capital is never idle. Agricultural output is produced according to a neoclassical constant returns to scale production function.

In the manufacturing sector, one unit of output can be produced by one worker and one unit of capital. However, it takes time and effort for idle factors to find each other. In other words, search is required to find employment and/or fill a vacancy. Once capital and labor are matched, a partnership is created that lasts until either the worker retires or capital becomes obsolete (each of these events occurs with an exogenously given probability, r, in each period). If the partnership dissolves, the remaining factor resumes searching. While the partnership lasts, the output produced is sold and the proceeds are distributed to labor and capital according to a sharing rule that is negotiated at the time the partnership forms.

The probability of successful search in the manufacturing sector depends on the mix of the searching population. Let s denote the fraction of searchers who are workers, $e(s)$ the per period probability that an unemployed worker finds a job, and $k(s)$ the per period probability that a vacancy is filled. Then if s increases, i.e., the unemployment pool becomes more labor intensive, it becomes harder to find employment but easier to fill a vacancy, i.e., $e'(s)<0$ and $k'(s)>0$. Since unemployment occurs only in the manufacturing sector, the equilibrium unemployment rate is tied to the size of the manufacturing sector and the value of s. The search technology is represented by $e(s)$ and $k(s)$.

Equilibrium occurs when the agricultural factor rewards adjust to clear the agricultural input markets, product prices adjust to clear product markets, and, since factors of production are mobile across sectors, labor and capital are distributed such that the expected lifetime return (in terms of income) from searching for employment in the manufacturing sector is equal to the lifetime income earned by working in the agricultural sector. This last condition is necessary since, for example, if the lifetime return to labor is higher in one sector than the other, all labor will flow to the high-income sector and no output will be produced in the remaining sector (implying an excess demand for output in at least one product market).

By examining the decision process of a typical worker seeking employment, we can see how income and congestion externalities distort incentives. We can also contrast this model with the reservation wage models discussed above. Consider first the position of a jobless worker seeking employment in the agricultural sector. Let w denote the agricultural wage. Then, since the agricultural labor market is frictionless, this worker will immediately find employment and earn w in each period until retiring. Since r represents the probability of retiring in any given period, $\frac{1}{r}$ is the expected length of time the worker remains employed. It follows that expected lifetime income is $\frac{w}{r}$.

Turn next to workers currently searching for employment in the manufacturing sector. Let P denote the revenue generated by the sale of a unit of manufacturing output and θ represent labor's share of revenue. In addition, let V_e denote expected lifetime income for a worker currently employed in manufacturing and V_u represent expected lifetime income for a searcher. Then V_e and V_u satisfy

$$V_e = \theta P + [1 - r]\{(1 - r)V_e + rV_u\}$$

$$V_u = (1 - r)\{e(s)V_e + [1 - e(s)]V_u\}$$

The first equation states that an employed worker's expected lifetime income is equal to current compensation (θP) plus expected future compensation provided that the worker does not retire (an event occurring with probability $1 - r$). Expected future consumption is equal to the probability that the capital used by the worker does not become obsolete ($[1 - r]$) multiplied by expected lifetime income while employed (V_e) plus the probability the job dissolves (r) multiplied by the expected lifetime income of an unemployed worker (V_u). The second equation states that expected lifetime income for an unemployed worker is equal to the probability of not retiring multiplied by a weighted average of income if employed and income if unemployed where the weights are equal to the probabilities of being in that state in the next period (I assume unemployment compensation is zero). These two equations can be solved for V_e and V_u to obtain the benefit due to employment

$$V_e - V_u = \frac{\theta P}{1 - (1 - r)(1 - r - e)}.$$

Note that regardless of the value of θ, $V_e - V_u > 0$ so that, in contrast to the reservation wage model, searchers never turn down job offers. This immediately implies that the duration of unemployment simply depends on the amount of time it takes to find an idle piece of capital. The search technology, $e(s)$, drives the model.

A similar analysis can be carried out to determine the expected lifetime return to capital if in use (V_k) and when idle (V_i). For any value of θ, it can be shown that $V_k > V_i$ so that firms with vacancies never turn away workers seeking employment.

We are now in a position to describe the income and congestion externalities. Consider the problem faced by an unemployed worker trying to decide where to seek employment. If the worker applies for work in the agricultural sector, employment will be gained immediately and the worker can expect to earn $\frac{w}{r}$ before retiring. If employment in the manufacturing sector is sought, the worker enters the sector as a searcher and can expect to earn V_u before retiring. If $\frac{w}{r} > V_u$, then all workers will seek employment in the agricultural sector, no output will be produced in the manufacturing sector, and there will be excess demand for the manufactured goods. A similar argument rules out the possibility that $\frac{w}{r} < V_u$. Therefore, in equilibrium, workers distribute themselves such that $\frac{w}{r} = V_u$. Does this equilibrium condition imply an efficient allocation of labor resources across sectors? The answer is no. A worker who contemplates entering the search sector takes into account the fact that each job offer accepted raises expected lifetime income from V_u to V_e. However, the worker ignores the fact that accepting the job also increases the expected return on the capital used from V_i to V_k. Therefore, workers ignore a positive externality associated with entering the search sector and too few of them seek employment in the manufacturing sector. Of course, capital also ignores the positive external effect its entry into the search sector has on worker income so that there is too little capital involved in manufacturing as well. In summary, these income externalities result in a search sector that is too small and, since unemployment is positively related to the size of the manufacturing sector, there is too much unemployment in equilibrium.

Congestion externalities arise due to the fact that the entry and/or exit of factors from manufacturing alters the value of s and therefore the employment probabilities. An extra worker seeking employment raises s, lowers the probability that other workers will find employment, and makes it easier to fill a vacancy. Davidson, Martin, and Matusz demonstrate that because of these congestion externalities, the search sector is too asymmetric in equilibrium. In other words, if $s > \frac{1}{2}$ so that the searching population is labor-intensive, then efficiency would be enhanced by making the sector more capital-intensive. If $s < \frac{1}{2}$, then the performance of the economy would be improved by making the sector more labor-intensive. Loosely, if $s > \frac{1}{2}$, then, when a worker enters the search sector, the negative externalities imposed on fellow workers outweigh the positive externalities enjoyed by capital, since labor is in the majority. Thus, the overall effect is that the sector is too labor-intensive. What are the implications for unemployment? The matching technology works best when the sector is perfectly symmetric. With an equal number of factors on both sides of the market, there are no excess vacancies or searchers; the only problem in creating jobs is getting the idle factors together. Therefore, when the sector is too asymmetric the matching technology is not being used efficiently and jobs are lost. The implication is that congestion externalities lead to too much unemployment.

In summary, the Davidson, Martin, and Matusz analysis suggests that, in general, income and congestion externalities work in opposite directions.[21] Unemployment may be too high or too low. Public policy specifically aimed at eliminating the external effects will enhance efficiency but may, in some instances, do so by increasing unemployment. I return to this issue in the policy section below.

Finally, before moving on to discuss some other insights provided by this literature, I wish to point out some features of the Davidson, Martin, and Matusz model that reflect the difference between the trade friction and reservation wage approaches. First, as stressed above, all job offers are accepted and unemployment simply depends on the rate at which firms and workers meet. The number of new jobs created depends on how well the market uses the search technology, a factor influenced by the equilibrium composition of the unemployment pool (as reflected in the value of s). Second, the trade friction model yields clear-cut, clean results and is easy to work with. There is no need to introduce heterogeneity across firms or workers in order to generate an equilibrium level of unemployment. As we will see below, this makes policy analysis much less complicated than it would be in a model following the reservation wage approach.

(ii) Multiple Equilibria, Feedback Mechanisms, and Business Cycles

When externalities distort incentives, government policies can be used to alter incentives at the margin and guide the economy back towards optimality. If equilibrium is unique, this is all the government intervention that is required or desired. If, however, more than one equilibrium exists, additional policies may be needed to insure that the economy ends up in the "best" equilibrium. Peter Diamond has demonstrated that this is a problem that is likely to emerge when trading frictions are present (see, for example, Diamond 1984b). To be more precise, Diamond has shown that models with search-generated unemployment are likely to be characterized by multiple equilibria. This result asserts that there may be more than one equilibrium rate of unemployment, i.e., more than one "natural rate of unemployment" and is consistent with the Keynesian notion that the economy can get "stuck" in an equilibrium in which output remains below its full employment level. The reason for this is simple. In equilibrium, each firm is maximizing profits and has no desire to increase its labor force. Now, consider what would occur if *all* firms simultaneously increased their recruiting efforts, increased their labor forces, and increased production. The increase in employment would generate a larger level of worker income, thereby increasing the demand for output. If the increased demand in the product market is large enough, it could justify the increased recruiting efforts. Therefore, a new equilibrium with lower unemployment might be established. Note that in the original equilibrium, by definition, no individual firm has an incentive to alter employment.

However, if recruiting efforts could be coordinated across all firms so that all firms simultaneously increase employment, the increased hiring is profitable. The force at work here is called a "feedback mechanism." Simply put, the increase in labor market activity stimulates demand in the product market which, in turn, feeds back to the labor market by increasing labor demand. When the original increase in hiring exactly matches the generated increase in labor demand, a new equilibrium is established.

Diamond also demonstrates that economies characterized by multiple equilibria may exhibit interesting dynamic behavior. This follows from the fact that current search behavior depends on the type of equilibrium agents expect to occur in the future. For example, if agents expect the economy to be booming in the future, then the return to search will be large and it makes sense to search relatively intensely. If, on the other hand, agents expect a recession, the return to current search is likely to be low (it will be very hard to find employment) and search activity will fall off. In each case, expectations are self-fulfilling in that increased (decreased) search activity increases (decreases) the number of new jobs created. Greater (less) employment translates into greater (less) income and implies a more (less) prosperous economy. Since expectations play such an important role in the evolution of the economy, waves of pessimism and optimism sweeping across the country can generate dynamics that look very much like a business cycle.

A brief review of a simple version of the Diamond model helps to crystalize these results and also lays a foundation for a discussion of policy-related issues in the next section. The model is extremely simple, yet it captures the fundamental elements of production and exchange in a friction-filled environment. There are no firms; instead, workers search for a suitable "production opportunity." When such an opportunity arises, the worker produces output and then attempts to trade it for goods that he or she can consume.

Production opportunities arrive at a constant rate but vary in their cost. Workers undertake low-cost projects but shun high-cost ones. The break-even cost, i.e., the cost at which the worker is indifferent between continuing to search for a lower-cost project and producing, is the worker's "reservation cost." The reservation cost plays the same role that the reservation wage plays in standard labor market search analysis: a higher reservation cost implies that the worker is more willing to accept a job.

Once production occurs, the worker must search for a trading partner. The reason for this is that workers are not allowed to consume goods that they themselves have produced. This assumption captures the notion that, in reality, people tend to specialize in production and generalize in consumption. Trading becomes easier as production increases, since there are more agents to trade with. Once trade takes place, the workers consume the output and then begin searching for new production opportunities. Workers are characterized as "unemployed" when engaged in search for a low-cost project and "employed" when searching for a trading partner.

As we will see below, the key assumption is that trade becomes easier as production increases. This amounts to an assumption that the search technology is characterized by increasing returns to scale and it is the driving force behind the result that equilibrium is not unique.

The entire model can be characterized by two equations. The first is an equilibrium condition stating that, in a steady state equilibrium, the flows into and out of employment must be equal so that unemployment remains constant. The second equation defines optimal search effort in the labor market given the current economic environment. When both equations are satisfied, the economy is in a steady state equilibrium.

Begin with the equilibrium condition. Let E denote current employment, N the size of the labor force, $B(E)$ the probability of finding a trading partner at any point in time, c^* the reservation cost, $G(c)$ the cumulative probability distribution for the cost of production; and z the probability of finding a production project. By assumption, as employment (E) increases, it becomes easier to find a trading partner (this is the increasing returns to scale assumption). Thus, $B'(E) > 0$. Consider first the flow from employment into unemployment. Employed workers are those who are looking for someone to trade output with. They become unemployed by locating a trading partner and carrying out an exchange of goods. Since E represents employment and $B(E)$ is the probability of locating a trading partner, $EB(E)$ equals the number of workers entering the unemployment pool at each instant. Turn next to the transition from unemployment to employment. At each point in time, $N - E$ workers are unemployed (looking for a low-cost production opportunity). With probability z a jobless worker is offered a project, and with probability $G(c^*)$ the project is acceptable (its cost is below the worker's reservation cost). Thus, $(N - E)zG(c^*)$ unemployed workers become employed at each instant.[22] Finally, let $\dot{E}$ denote the change in employment at each instant. If $\dot{E} > 0$ employment is increasing, and if $\dot{E} < 0$, unemployment is increasing. It follows that

(7) $\dot{E} = (N - E)zG(c^*) - EB(E)$.

We are in a steady state when $\dot{E} = 0$.

Equation (7) is depicted in figure 2.2. As c^* rises, workers are more willing to undertake production projects (i.e., accept jobs) and the flow from unemployment to employment increases. To restore equilibrium ($\dot{E} = 0$), the flow out of employment must also increase. For this to occur, it must become easier to find a trading partner; that is, E must rise (so that $B(E)$ increases). Therefore, the combinations of E and c^* that are consistent with steady state equilibrium in the labor market are represented by an upward sloping curve (the $\dot{E} = 0$ curve in figure 2.2). Above this curve c^* is too large for equilibrium (for a given value of E), implying that workers are too willing to accept jobs. Therefore, the flow into employment exceeds the flow out and employment is increasing. Below the curve, $\dot{E} < 0$.

Turn next to the determination of c^*. Workers will be more willing to undertake high-cost projects when they expect it to be relatively easy to trade their output, since this would allow them to consume the output and reenter the labor market quickly. Due to the assumption of increasing returns to scale in the search technology, trade becomes easier as E rises. Thus, c^* is an increasing function of E, as depicted by the $c^*(E)$ curve in figure 2.2. This curve would be horizontal under constant returns to scale.

Since workers choose c^* (to maximize expected lifetime income), the economy *always* operates along this curve regardless of whether or not it is in a steady state equilibrium. If the current level of employment is such that the $c^*(E)$ curve lies above the $\dot{E} = 0$ curve, then employment increases and the economy moves up to the right along $c^*(E)$. If employment is such that $c^*(E)$ lies below the $\dot{E} = 0$ curve, then employment falls and the economy slides down $c^*(E)$ towards the origin. The economy is in a steady state equilibrium when $\dot{E} = 0$ along the $c^*(E)$ curve. Since both curves are upward sloping, they may intersect any number of times. As drawn in figure 2.2 there are several equilibria, one for each intersection of the two curves.[23] The existence of more than one equilibrium is a direct result of the feedback mechanism described above and the assumption of increasing returns to scale in the search technology. If workers expect it to be easier to trade output, they are more willing to undertake costly projects. The greater willingness to accept jobs results in greater output which, in turn, does indeed make it easier to trade (*if* there are increasing returns to scale in the search technology). Hence, the worker's original optimism is warranted. However, pessimism can also be warranted. If all workers expect it to be difficult to trade output, they will be reluctant to accept high-cost projects. This unwillingness to produce implies a low level of output and makes it hard to find a trading partner. Diamond demonstrates that changes in expectations about the future environment can cause the economy to bounce back and forth between high- and low-employment equilibria in a manner that closely resembles the business cycle.[24] Note that with constant returns to scale such business cycle behavior could not arise, since equilibrium would be unique ($c^*(E)$ and $\dot{E} = 0$ intersect only once when $c^*(E)$ is horizontal).

As is clear from figure 2.2, unemployment varies across the equilibria. The "best" equilibrium, in terms of welfare, is the one with the lowest level of unemployment. It is not clear, however, that the economy will naturally gravitate towards this equilibrium without government intervention. Moreover, even if the economy did manage to reach the best equilibrium, the existence of congestion externalities implies that even the high-employment equilibrium is suboptimal—welfare could be enhanced even further by implementing policies aimed at increasing workers' willingness to accept production opportunities.

Figure 2.2

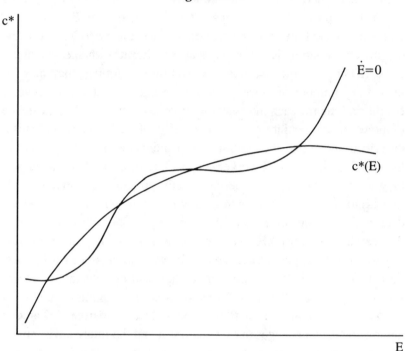

Although the Diamond model is extremely simple, it captures what appear to be the most important features of economies troubled by search-generated unemployment. These features include the fact that it takes time and effort to find trading opportunities (in both input and product markets), the importance of expectations concerning the future economic environment in making present search-related decisions (e.g., how hard should workers search and/or how many resources should firms devote to recruitment?), and the fact that search decisions made by an individual affect the welfare of others. Diamond's analysis is important because it demonstrates that even in a simple barter economy with no firms these features can produce several striking results, e.g., multiple equilibria that can be Pareto-ranked and business cycles. The intuition offered at the beginning of this subsection suggests that these results will continue to emerge in more elaborate models that more closely resemble our economy.

(iii) The Value of a Job

Total national income is one measure of welfare that is often used to evaluate the desirability of certain policies. In a standard neoclassical general equilibrium model, total national income is equal to the value of output. Consequently, the value of a job is captured fully by the value of the output it produces and the level and composition of employment do not enter the welfare function. Davidson, Martin, and Matusz (1987b, 1989) have shown that this is not the case when workers are finitely lived and trading frictions are present. In such an environment, jobs carry with them a surplus value above and beyond the value of the output they produce. Furthermore, the size of the surplus is tied to the expected duration of unemployment required to find the job. This implies that the number and types of jobs held in equilibrium must be considered when evaluating policies aimed at increasing welfare.

To illustrate this point, return to the Davidson, Martin, and Matusz model outlined above and make one small change; assume that workers leave the workforce due to death rather than retirement and that newly born workers enter the labor force at a rate that keeps the number of labor force participants constant over time. In this model, the value of a manufacturing job can be shown to be equal to the value of the output it produces *plus* $Z \equiv V_e - V_u + V_k - V_i$. Z is a measure of the surplus value of each job and is equal to the increase in expected income attained by labor and capital when the job is created.

If we let J denote the steady state number of jobs held in the search sector, then total welfare is equal to the value of output plus JZ. Two points are worth making. First, the number of search sector jobs held in equilibrium matters. Since search sector jobs carry with them a surplus value while agricultural jobs do not, manufacturing jobs are more valuable to society. Second, the harder a manufacturing job is to obtain, the larger is its surplus value. This follows from the fact that jobs that are more difficult to obtain generate a larger difference between V_e and V_u.[25] This is precisely why agricultural jobs carry no surplus value. In any given sector, V_e and V_u will differ only if a spell of unemployment is required to find a job. But, this is not the case in the agricultural sector, since its factor markets are frictionless. The implication is that the composition of jobs also matters. In an economy with several search sectors, jobs that are more difficult to obtain carry with them a larger surplus value.

Why are some jobs more valuable than others? To answer this question, consider the labor market experience of a cohort of newly born workers. When they are born, a number of workers choose to seek employment in the manufacturing sector. Since they begin their search unemployed, they can each expect to earn V_u over their lifetime. The remainder take jobs in the agricultural sector and can expect to earn $\frac{w}{r}$ before death. Therefore, at birth, expected lifetime income for this cohort is equal to $MV_u + A\frac{w}{r}$, where M refers to the number seeking search sector jobs and A represents those taking agricultural jobs. A similar expression can be derived for the return to new capital. It can be shown that these terms sum to a number that is equal to the value of steady-state output. Therefore, each newly born generation of workers can expect to earn income exactly equal to the value of steady-state output—no more or less. This implies that the interests of future generations of workers are best served by implementing policies aimed at maximizing the value of output.

Now, as this generation of workers matures, they begin to find employment in the manufacturing sector. With each job accepted, welfare increases by the surplus value of the job. At maturity, J manufacturing jobs are held and welfare is equal to the value of output plus JZ. This implies that the interests of current mature generations are best served by implementing policies aimed at maximizing the value of output plus the surplus value of jobs. The interests of current and future generations diverge. We discuss this point in greater detail in the policy section below.

Intuitively, workers currently employed realize that they may lose their jobs and be forced to search for new employment in the future.

If this occurs, their new job may entail using capital that has not yet entered the input market. Since they share the proceeds of production with the capital they use, this implies that part of expected lifetime income is generated by using factors of production not currently in use. In other words, the surplus arises because current generations borrow from the future each time a search-sector job is created. The greater the number of steady-state jobs, the more current generations can borrow from the future. It is important to note that this borrowing is not at the expense of future generations. After all, as mentioned above, future generations can expect to earn income exactly equal to the value of the output they produce regardless of the number of search-sector jobs. Moreover, as this future generation matures, it also borrows from the unborn. Of course, the surplus value of jobs would not appear if workers were infinitely lived since, in that case, borrowing from the future is equivalent to borrowing from yourself.

(iv) Limitations

Even though the trade friction approach was developed less than 10 years ago, it has already yielded an impressive number of insights. In terms of the model introduced in section A, it has allowed us to address the question of whether or not the natural rate of unemployment is efficient (taking as given the process by which firms and workers meet) in a fairly simple setting. This has been accomplished by focusing on how the market manages to determine e, the job-finding rate, by creating incentives for firms and workers to enter the search process and expend effort to find employment. We have seen that market externalities lead to an inefficient job-finding rate and that feedback mechanisms may create more than one equilibrium. Unfortunately, very little effort has been made to use this approach to explain how jobs dissolve.[26] The separation rate, s, is almost always taken as exogenous in these models. This is disturbing in light of the fact that there is strong empirical evidence that most unemployed workers become unemployed involuntarily (through layoffs).[27] A good theory of unemployment needs to explain why layoffs occur.

It should be fairly easy to extend the trade friction models in a manner that allows for endogenous job separations. One can easily imagine a model with several search sectors in which exogenous shocks cause prices to fluctuate across sectors. As price falls in a particular sector, the value of each match in that sector drops and may fall below the expected return from search in another sector. This would cause the firm to lay off the worker. Unfortunately, the worker would also wish to sever the relationship, and thus such a model would not be able to explain *involuntary* job separations. In addition, such a model would be unable to explain the source of the exogenous shocks. A theory about cyclical fluctuations in unemployment should be able to explain the origin of business cycles as well as their implications for the labor market. Therefore, for search theory to continue to evolve as a major theory of unemployment, we need to find ways to extend the model to allow for layoff unemployment and business cycles. For a more detailed discussion of these issues, interested readers are referred to Pissarides (1988) on the issue of layoffs and Howitt and McAfee (1988) on endogenous business cycles.

E. Employment Policies, Unemployment and Efficiency

My goal in this section is to examine a number of policies commonly used to deal with the unemployment problem using the framework provided by the search literature. The treatment offered here is in no way meant to represent a complete analysis of the impact of these policies; instead, it reflects the insights that the search literature provides with respect to each program.

The discussion focuses on two related issues: the impact of the program on unemployment and efficiency. We consider these issues separately since, as discussed above, there are cases in which a reduction in unemployment does not signal an increase in efficiency. Nonetheless, policymakers often have noneconomic objectives in mind and may be more interested in reducing unemployment than in achieving allocative efficiency. Moreover, it is not difficult to imagine that some politicians might find the concept that an increase in unemployment is necessary to improve efficiency politically unpalatable. Finally, when assessing the potential value of a policy on efficiency grounds, it will be useful to divide social welfare into two components: the value of output and the surplus value from employment.

(i) Transfer Payment, Unemployment and Duration

In terms of job search, government programs that make payments directly to individuals can be separated into two categories: those that provide income to the unemployed and those that supplement the income of the employed (or newly employed). Payments to unemployed searchers, such as unemployment insurance, reduce the cost of joblessness and therefore make search relatively more attractive. In a model with a distribution of wages, this results in higher reservation wages. If the wage offer distribution remains unchanged, unemployment and duration both rise. However, as shown by Albrecht and Axell (1984), it is possible for the wage-offer distribution to shift in a manner that actually reduces unemployment (see the discussion in section C.ii above).

The trade friction approach also suggests that such policies will increase unemployment. If, for example, workers choose search effort to maximize expected lifetime utility, then any increase in search costs will lead to a decrease in aggregate search effort. This triggers increases in both the level and duration of unemployment. In fact, even with search effort fixed, the link still exists. To see this, consider a multisector model in which the structure and level of unemployment varies across sectors. In equilibrium, all active sectors will have to offer workers the same expected lifetime income (otherwise, searchers will simply flow to the sector offering the highest expected return and the remaining sectors will produce no output). Sectors with the highest unemployment rate will therefore have to offer higher wages in order to compensate workers for the relatively longer spells of unemployment they would face in such sectors. Since payments to searchers make unemployment less costly, they result in more searchers seeking jobs in these high-paying sectors. This, in turn, increases the economywide unemployment rate (see Davidson, Martin, and Matusz 1987b for details). Of course, policies that reduce the wages of the employed, such as wage taxes, generate exactly the same type of effects.

Considering the results from the trade friction literature, the insights offered by the early partial-partial equilibrium models, and the evidence that wage offers are rarely rejected (so that the importance of the Albrecht/Axell finding is diminished), it seems reasonable to conclude that policies subsidizing unemployment or taxing employment should *theoretically* result in a drop in the number of jobs and increase the average spell of unemployment. With respect to unemployment insurance, these hypotheses have been confirmed empirically by a number of authors (see, for example, Topel 1983, 1984).

By similar arguments, programs offering additional compensation to the employed encourage search and reduce the unemployment rate. Briefly, increasing the reward associated with employment increases the return to search while making unemployment relatively less attractive than it would be in the absence of such a scheme. The result is a reduction in reservation wages, increased search effort, and an increased willingness to accept low-paying jobs. All three of these effects reduce both the average spell of unemployment and the unemployment rate. Policies that affect unemployment in this manner include job subsidies (subsidies to firms and employees paid at the time a new job is created), wages subsidies and programs that pay workers a bonus for finding employment in a relatively short, prespecified length of time. An example of the latter policy would be the bonus program in Illinois that paid newly unemployed workers $500 if they accepted a job during the first 11 weeks of unemployment. This experimental program produced results consistent with search theory: the duration of unemployment fell by a full week (see Woodbury and Spiegelman 1987 for details)!

The manner in which transfer programs are financed can also have an important impact on unemployment. For example, a number of authors have criticized the manner in which unemployment insurance (UI) is financed. UI is funded by a payroll tax levied on wages that fall below a given ceiling. This has important implications for unemployment. Because wages above a certain level are exempt from the tax, financing UI in this manner increases the incentives firms face to employ high-wage workers. Hamermesh (1977) has suggested raising the ceiling on distributional grounds and in order to reduce unemployment among low-wage workers. The argument runs as follows. Since firms pay relatively more in taxes when they hire low-wage workers, they offer them fewer "good jobs." By increasing the ceiling, the distortion is removed and low-wage workers should benefit. In an intriguing paper, Wright and Loberg (1987) demonstrate that, to some degree, Hamermesh's argument is correct but incomplete. In particular, they show that an increase in the ceiling lowers the reservation wages of low-wage workers, thereby reducing their unemployment rate. However, there are two caveats. First, the reservation wages and unemployment of high-wage workers both rise. Second, and perhaps most important, they show that the average wage earned by the low-wage workers (both before and after taxes) fall so that expected income falls when the ceiling is raised. Wright and Loberg therefore advocate, as an alternative policy, an increase in the tax ceiling accompanied by an equiproportionate reduction in the tax rate. They go on to demonstrate that such a policy change does not affect high-wage workers at all, while achieving the goal of increasing the employment and after-tax wages of low-wage workers.[28]

Finally, transfer payments and taxes may also have an important impact on the relative earnings of workers and firms. As discussed above, trade frictions create an environment in which wages are shielded from competitive labor market forces. Search costs, therefore, provide both firms and workers with a degree of monopoly power, resulting in a wage that depends on the relative bargaining power of the two contracting parties. For example, in a simple one-sector model Pissarides (1985) demonstrates that unemployment insurance increases the bargaining power of the potential employee, since it reduces search costs. This leads to an increase in wages and a reduction in profits. Proportional wage taxes paid by firms lower the worker's value to the firm. Consequently, the bargaining power of the firm is enhanced and its share of revenue rises.

(ii) Minimum Wages, Employment Agencies, and Aggregate Demand Management

Among the additional policies that affect unemployment, three in particular are worth discussing: minimum wage laws, state-run employment agencies and aggregate demand management. While traditional arguments in favor of minimum wage laws usually entail distributional issues, these latter two policies are specifically targeted at increasing employment.

Virtually any model of the labor market predicts that effective minimum wage laws will increase unemployment. Debate therefore usually centers on the question of whether the increase in income for low-wage workers is sufficient to justify the policy. However, multisector trade friction models reveal that these wage floors may also have important allocative effects (see Davidson, Martin, and Matusz 1988). Since, if labor is mobile, each sector must offer searchers the same expected return from search, low-wage sectors are characterized by less unemployment than high-wage sectors. Minimum wage laws increase the wages that firms in the low-unemployment sectors must pay, and this reduces the demand for labor by those firms. This further increases unemployment by reallocating labor towards the high-unemployment sectors. As in traditional models, the increased flow of searchers to the high-unemployment sectors causes the wages in this sector to fall and increases the average spell of unemployment.

Turn next to state-run employment agencies, where the goal is to reduce unemployment by improving the efficiency of the matching process. These agencies offer an alternative to the search process by registering and matching unemployed workers with firms carrying vacancies. Pissarides (1979) constructs a simple search model of the labor market in order to determine the optimal policies that state-run employment agencies should adopt if their goal is to increase employment. In his model, all unemployed workers must register with the agency in order to qualify for unemployment insurance. These workers may also engage in costly private search activity in order to further increase their likelihood of employment. Firms have a choice, they can either register their vacancy with the agency or advertise privately, but not both. This assumption is justified on empirical grounds (see Evans 1977). Firms receive no compensation from registering with the agency and do so only because it might be a quicker way to fill the position. Vacant jobs that are publicly advertised are available to all workers engaged in private search activity.

Pissarides derives several interesting results. Most important, he demonstrates that while a reduction in the cost of private search always reduces unemployment, policies that reduce the cost associated with using the employment agency have an ambiguous effect on employment. This follows from the fact that increased activity at the agency reduces the incentive to search privately. The fall in private search effort reduces employment and this effect might be sufficient to outweigh the increase in jobs brought about by the increased efficiency at the employment agency. As far as policy is concerned, this result indicates that the agency should employ methods that encourage private search activity. For example, rather than trying to entice more firms to register their vacancies (doing so would lower the return to private search), it is better to subsidize private job advertisements by firms. Alternatively, the government could charge workers a fee for using the agency or tie unemployment benefits to the number of contacts made with firms during the search period, i.e., the government could provide a bonus for each contact made. These policies would reduce the number of jobs generated by agency activity, but would increase employment overall.[29]

Finally, consider the role of aggregate demand management. As shown in section D.ii, the externalities inherent in the search process create a feedback mechanism that may lead to multiple equilibria. Which equilibrium the economy actually settles down to depends on the current level of economic activity and agents' expectations about future trading opportunities. Actions taken by the government to stimulate aggregate demand can lead the economy towards a more desired equilibrium (one with lower unemployment). This provides a rationale for the Keynesian policy of "pump priming." Furthermore, government programs designed to convince agents that the economic future is bright can also be an effective way to guide the economy towards the desired equilibrium. Propaganda can be beneficial!

(iii) Efficiency

The externalities inherent in the search process make it almost certain that the equilibrium level of unemployment will not be efficient. Unfortunately, search theory does not provide any clear-cut prescriptions for dealing with this problem. There are a number of reasons for this. First, as we have seen above, search activity simultaneously generates positive and negative external effects, so that it is impossible to know whether unemployment is too high or too low. Second, although it is by now accepted that such externalities exist, no one has yet been able to demonstrate that their effects are nontrivial. Are the distortions so small in size that they may be ignored, or are they large enough to warrant costly government corrective programs? Empirical work aimed at addressing this issue might also be helpful in pinpointing the dominate external effect, thereby addressing the first issue as well. Finally, as shown in the recent papers by Davidson, Martin, and Matusz (1987b, 1989) the combination of search and finite life creates an environment in which the interests of current and future generations diverge. Briefly, while the unborn prefer policies aimed at maximizing the value of steady-state output, current generations wish to maximize the *sum* of this value and the surplus value of the jobs held in equilibrium. Since the policies that maximize the value of output differ, in general, from those that maximize the surplus value from employment, these cohorts will generally prefer different policies. In fact, Davidson, Martin, and Matusz (1987b) demonstrate that there are cases in which the unborn desire unemployment insurance without job subsidies (to shift resources to the high-unemployment sector) while the current generation prefers the exact opposite!

In spite of these problems, the existence of a surplus value from employment does have policy implications that should not be ignored. In particular, jobs that are more durable and more difficult to obtain generate a larger social surplus than other jobs. All else equal, this implies that policies should be aimed at expanding low-turnover sectors in which it is difficult to secure employment. In the cases in which these jobs are also characterized by relatively high wages, as is likely to be the case (see Davidson, Martin, and Matusz 1990), this theory lends some support to recent calls for protection of high-wage industries.

Conclusions

Given these difficulties involved in tailoring policies to raise economic welfare and given that there seems to be a clear presumption (at least publically) that reducing unemployment is an important goal, it seems reasonable to conclude that policymakers will be most interested in what the search literature dictates along these lines. With this in mind, the most potent policies are those that promote search activity and remove trade frictions. Bonuses to workers finding employment, bonuses to searchers contacting firms, subsidies to firms advertising their vacancies, job and wage subsidies and, provided that they are run properly, state-run employment agencies are favored over programs such as minimum wage laws and unemployment insurance. There is a clear role for the government to act as an economic cheerleader, encouraging private economic activity by insisting that the future looks favorable and pumping up the economy by increasing aggregate demand if it appears headed in the wrong direction.

NOTES

1. Therefore, since both sides of the market are not modeled, it would be inappropriate to call it a partial equilibrium approach.
2. This nomenclature is borrowed from Pissarides (1988).
3. This model is adapted from Mortensen (1970).
4. See Mattila (1974).
5. See table B-41 of the 1987 Economic Report of the President.
6. See Topel (1983).
7. See table B-41 of the 1987 Economic Report of the President.

8. See Feldstein (1973) and Mortensen (1986).

9. See Lilien and Hall (1986) or Pissarides (1988).

10. The importance of the assumption that the wage-offer distribution is known is discussed in note 12 below.

11. It is interesting to note that for workers nearing retirement (or those facing liquidity constraints), the reservation wage falls over time. This follows from the fact that as retirement nears (or, as savings are depleted) additional search is less likely to be fruitful. Therefore, $G(w)$ falls over time, and the worker becomes more willing to accept a low-paying job. For young workers with adequate savings, the reservation wage remains constant over time.

12. An obvious weakness of this analysis is the assumption that workers know the wage-offer distribution with certainty before beginning to search. This is simply not the case. Workers learn of their potential value in the market by contacting firms and seeking employment. In other words, workers learn about the wage-offer distribution by sampling from it. It is therefore important to know whether optimal search from an unknown distribution is similar to that from a known distribution. A formal analysis of this issue was provided by Rothschild (1974) and the results are comforting. Assuming that the worker begins with an estimate of the distribution and updates this estimate as search occurs, Rothschild provided examples in which the optimal search strategy would be characterized by a reservation price rule. To obtain this result, it was necessary to use restrictions on the form of the original estimate and on the type of updating rule used as new information is obtained. Although the conditions appear restrictive, he argues (convincingly) in the conclusion that the basic result (the optimality of the reservation price rule) is probably far more general. Therefore, it seems the assumption that the wage-offer distribution is known is a useful abstraction that does not seriously limit the applicability of the model.

13. The empirical importance of relaxing this assumption is discussed in Barron (1975).

14. See also Gal, Landsberger and Levykson (1981), Morgan (1983), and Morgan and Manning (1985) for similar approaches.

15. See also Johnson (1978), Viscusi (1979), and Wilde (1979) for similar approaches. In these studies it is generally assumed that the worker does not know the quality of the job when hired. Over time, as he or she works, the quality of the job is revealed (i.e., jobs are experience goods) and if the match is poor, the worker quits. This yields a model very similar to Jovanovic's.

16. It is worth noting that, since equilibrium is characterized by all firms offering the same level of compensation, all job offers will be accepted. Unemployment is then simply tied to the rate at which the workers receive job offers, a factor that, as we will see below, the reservation wage approach makes little or no attempt to explain.

17. Albrecht and Axell do not present their result in this manner. Instead, they place restrictions on the productivity distribution to insure that unemployment rises with unemployment compensation. They also point out that a selective increase in unemployment compensation restricted to low-wage workers unambiguously reduces unemployment. Such a selective program does so by increasing the low wage and driving the least productive firms from the market. This increases the fraction of firms offering high wages and causes unemployment to fall. Note that this policy is costless, since low-wage workers are never unemployed and therefore never collect unemployment insurance.

18. See Diamond and Maskin (1979) for a notable exception.

19. For a review of the externalities involved in the search process, see Mortensen (1986) particularly section 4 and Hosios (1990).

20. Descriptions of congestion and income externalities can be found in many other papers including Diamond (1982b), Pissarides (1984a, 1984b), Mortensen (1986), and Hosios (1990). I have chosen to use the Davidson, Martin, and Matusz set-up due to my own obvious familiarity with the model.

21. It is important to remember that in this model, search intensity is not allowed to vary. When search intensity is endogenous, the externalities lead to further distortions. Income externalities lead to a search intensity that is too low (implying too much unemployment), while congestion externalities have ambiguous effects.

22. Note that in this model, unlike the one developed by Davidson, Martin, and Matusz, workers still reject some job offers (since some projects cost more than c^*). However, none of Diamond's results depend on the form of $G(c)$, and therefore his results are not driven by the rate of job rejection. As with most trade friction models, it is the search technology ($B(E)$) that drives the model.

23. There is an additional equilibrium at the origin where no production takes place, because workers are unwilling to undertake even the lowest-cost projects ($c^* = 0$). This is an equilibrium since, if no one else is producing, there will be no one for a worker to trade with if he or she chooses to produce. Thus, there is an equilibrium in which everyone is unemployed.

24. Changes in expectations actually cause the $c^*(E)$ curve to shift, altering the equilibria and, as Diamond shows, may change the type of equilibrium the economy heads towards.

25. To see this, note that in section (i) we derived $V_e - V_u$ and it was decreasing in e, the job-finding rate.

26. See Jovanovic (1983) for a notable exception.

27. See Topel (1983) and Lilien and Hall (1986).

28. The fact that UI is "experience rated" has also drawn a great deal of criticism, mostly because this feature contributes to layoff unemployment. The forces at work in this instance have little to do with search and will be discussed in detail in the chapter on contracts. The interested reader is also referred to Brechling (1981) or Topel (1983).

29. This does not imply that it would be optimal to do away with the agency altogether. In fact, Pissarides shows that such policies work only if all workers remain registered with the agency. In addition, if all workers engage in private search activity, then it is optimal to encourage firms to register their vacancies.

3
Non-Walrasian Equilibria

Prior to the late 1960s, virtually all microeconomic models included the assumption that prices were perfectly flexible and able to adjust instantaneously to equate supply and demand. No rigorous explanation was offered for how prices would adjust when out of equilibrium; it was simply assumed that some dynamic process would lead us instantly to the market-clearing values. The continued reliance on this assumption led to (what I consider) the three most embarrassing facts about the state of economic theory. First, with perfectly flexible prices and frictionless markets, involuntary unemployment (by definition) cannot occur at a positive wage rate. Therefore, even though unemployment is considered a major barometer of economic performance in Western cultures, most economists have worked with models in which unemployment was a logical impossibility. Second, our models could not explain how the economy would adjust when out of equilibrium. There are a number of good reasons to be bothered by this. For example, microeconomics tells us that the selfish pursuit of private gain will result, under certain conditions, in an equilibrium that is Pareto Optimal. However, it does not tell us if this same selfish pursuit will lead us towards equilibrium if, for some reason, the equilibrium is disturbed. Nor does it tell us how selfishness leads us to equilibrium in the first place. Another problem arises from the fact that by ignoring out-of-equilibrium behavior, we necessarily ignore some important interactions in the marketplace. If prices adjust instantaneously, consumers and firms know that they will be able to complete all desired transactions. There is no need to take into account possible market constraints such as unemployment (which constrains worker income) or insufficient market demand (which constrains the firm's sales). These constraints link markets in important ways that equilibrium models effectively rule out (e.g., greater unemployment lowers workers income and reduces product market demand; smaller than expected sales cause firms to reduce their demand for inputs in factor markets).

The final embarrassment concerns the difference between macro- and microeconomics. Macroeconomics is the study of the economy at an aggregate level, with a particular emphasis on the determinants of economic activity (including unemployment) and the price level. Microeconomics is the study of individual behavior. One would expect these two fields to be linked, with micro models serving as the basis for macro theories. Unfortunately, since traditional microtheory relies on the assumption of perfectly flexible prices, there is no role for unemployment in such models. This has forced us to develop one set of theories to explain individual behavior and a different set of theories to explain behavior in the aggregate. One would have hoped for more consistency than this in a field that is over two hundred years old!

If we think carefully about the development of macroeconomics, it is easy to see the source of our difficulty in dealing with these issues. Modern macroeconomics was born with the publication of Keynes's "General Theory" in 1936. At that time, the theory of individual behavior was fairly well established. Although its mathematical formulation by Samuelson (1947) and Arrow and Debreu (1954) had not yet taken place, its reliance on market-clearing prices was firmly entrenched. Keynes's theories were difficult to integrate into this framework. He wrote of involuntary unemployment, a concept at odds with market clearing, and consumption as a function of *income,* a variable that should be endogenous (not a parameter) according to classical microeconomics. Due to the power of Keynes's theory and the seeming inconsistency between his theories and microeconomics, macroeconomics made little attempt to ground itself in true microeconomic principles.[1]

The "fixed-price" or "disequilibriium" models of the late sixties and early seventies, e.g., Clower (1965), Leijonhufvud (1968), and Barro and Grossman (1971, 1976), attempted to deal with these issues by providing a microeconomic framework in which Keynesian notions such as the consumption function and involuntary unemployment made sense.[2] This was done by assuming that prices were fixed (or slow to adjust) and by focusing on how the economy would behave when out of equilibrium. The fixed-price assumption was made for two related reasons. First, it is obvious that in reality prices do not always clear markets. Queues form every day in response to excess demand and firms are often forced to carry unplanned inventories. Such quantity adjustments determine which transactions will take place in the short run and it is only later, in the long run, that prices adjust. It therefore makes sense to ask how economies adjust when rigid, nonmarket-clearing prices prevail.

The second reason for focusing on fixed-price models is that it can be shown that links across markets are created by non-Walrasian prices that can provide a basis for certain Keynesian phenomena. These links can be described as follows. When prices are incorrect, one side of the market will not be able to carry out all desired transactions. Constraints faced by agents on the short side in one market obviously affect their behavior in other markets. For example, workers who fail to find a job reveal a different demand for goods than they would have if they had been able to secure employment. Changes in behavior caused by market constraints are known as ''quantity adjustments.'' These quantity adjustments interact and produce an equilibrium state even when prices are at nonmarket-clearing levels. The type of equilibrium created, however, behaves very differently from a standard Walrasian equilibrium. In fact, non-Walrasian equilibria may be characterized by involuntary unemployment. Moreover, Keynesian features such as multipliers and a consumption function with income as a parameter arise naturally in such an environment. Therefore, micro models with rational, utility-maximizing agents facing incorrect prices can provide a solid microeconomic foundation for Keynesian macroeconomic theory.

The goal of this chapter is to review the major insights provided by the fixed-price literature. This will be accomplished in three steps. In section A, I begin by explaining the difference between quantity and price adjustment in a partial equilibrium setting. When focusing on only one market, this is equivalent to the distinction between Walrasian and Marshallian stability. The analysis is extended to a general equilibrium framework in section B. The focus in this section is on the manner in which quantity adjustments link markets and produce non-Walrasian equilibria. I also stress that the effectiveness of various policies aimed at reducing unemployment depends on the types of quantity constraints faced by workers and firms.

In section B, prices are assumed to be fixed while quantities are allowed to adjust to clear markets. In section C, I discuss recent contributions aimed at providing a more complete theory in which prices are chosen by profit-maximizing firms with market induced constraints in mind. In some of the early studies, prices change from period to period with quantities adjusting within each period to achieve equilibrium. This effectively amounts to an assumption that while both prices and quantities react to market signals, quantity adjustments occur faster than price adjustments. More recent contributions have abandoned this assumption by allowing for simultaneous price and quantity determination. The main goal of this literature is to address the question of whether or not the selfish pursuit of private gain will necessarily lead towards the Walrasian equilibrium. One of the major results is that such models are often characterized by multiple equilibria that can be Pareto-ranked. The Walrasian equilibrium may be included in the set of equilibria but there is no guarantee that an unaided economy will end up at the Walrasian prices. This result is therefore qualitatively similar to those obtained by Peter Diamond in the search literature (see the previous chapter). The reason for the similarity is also discussed in section C.

A. Quantity vs. Price Adjustment

Suppose that, for some reason, a market is temporarily out of equilibrium. Will the economy adjust and move us towards equilibrium or are there market forces present that may actually push us away from equilibrium? To answer this question, two different adjustment processes have been proposed. The first, due to Leon Walras, assumes that prices adjust to equate supply and demand. The argument runs along the following lines. Suppose that price exceeds its market-clearing level so that the quantity supplied exceeds the quantity demanded (see figure 3.1).

Could this situation persist over time? The obvious answer to this question is no, since firms would build up ever increasing inventories as some of their goods remained unsold. In an effort to reduce inventories, firms would eventually be forced to lower their prices toward equilibrium. If, on the other hand, the price level is such that demand exceeds supply, either unsatisfied customers would bid up the price or firms would take advantage of the excess demand by raising price. In each case, price moves towards equilibrium. Eventually, the market-clearing price is reached and equilibrium is achieved.

Figure 3.1

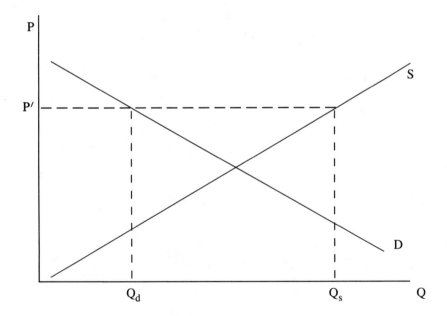

The alternative adjustment process, due to Alfred Marshall, actually predates Walras's theory and relies on quantity adjustments to clear markets. To explain how equilibrium is achieved, refer to figure 3.2. Suppose first that too little output has been produced. Then, according to the supply curve, the lowest price that suppliers are willing to accept for an additional unit of output (the "supply price") is P_s. This price is lower than P_d, the maximum price consumers are willing to pay for an additional unit of the product (the "demand price"). Since consumers are willing to pay more for extra output than firms are asking, firms respond by increasing output. This moves us closer to the equilibrium (or market-clearing) quantity. A similar argument can be used to show that if too much output is produced (so that the supply price exceeds the demand price) market forces lead firms to reduce output. Once again, although for different reasons, the market works—when out of equilibrium the market adjusts and moves us back towards equilibrium.

Figure 3.2

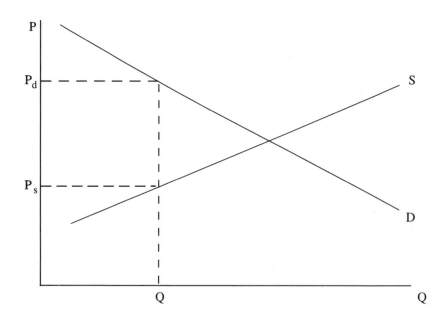

In a partial equilibrium setting, the distinction between price and quantity adjustment processes may seem like a distinction without a difference. After all, in each case the outcome is the same: the market ends up in equilibrium with supply equaling demand. This would not be the case, however, if, for some reason, demand or supply were perversely sloped. For example, in figure 3.3a it can be shown that the equilibrium is stable under the Walrasian price adjustment process but unstable when Marshallian quantity adjustment is assumed. The opposite is true for figure 3.3b. Therefore, at least in some cases, the assumed adjustment process matters.

While this analysis has provided insight into the difference between quantity and price adjustment, and although these arguments have been used countless times in the literature to address the question of stability, the reasoning behind each argument is flawed. To begin with, both stories of out-of-equilibrium adjustments are just that—stories. No one has developed a model of profit-maximizing price-setting firms and demonstrated that it is in their interest to raise price in the presence of excess demand and lower price when facing excess supply. Although this seems intuitively plausible and although a great deal of effort has been expended to demonstrate its truthfulness, to date no one has been successful.[3] Likewise, no one has demonstrated that the most profitable course of action is to increase output when the demand price exceeds the supply price. Therefore, neither theory of adjustment has been shown to be consistent with profit or utility-maximizing behavior.

A more serious flaw with the analyses rests in the fact that, although both theories purport to tell us how agents act in disequilibrium, they rely on supply and demand curves that are generated under the assumption that all desired transactions can be completed. For example, the labor demand schedule is derived by maximizing profits under the assumption that all output produced can be sold. If, as may be the case if prices are incorrect, there is insufficient demand in the product market, the firm will reveal a different demand for labor. Supply and demand curves derived under the assumption that agents will not be constrained in carrying out transactions are known as "notional." Demand and supply curves derived taking into account the quantity constraints generated by nonmarket-clearing prices are known as "effective." The

Figure 3.3a

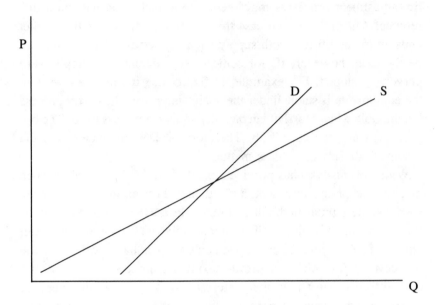

Figure 3.3b

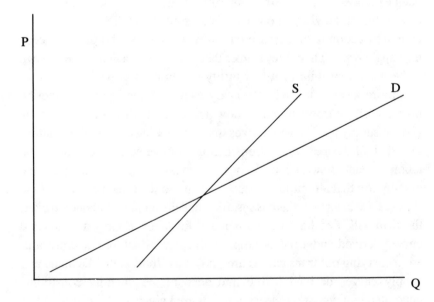

analyses above focus on notional demand and supply. However, if the economy is not in equilibrium, it is the effective demand and supply curves that govern matters.

To derive the effective demands, we need to know which agents are constrained in the remaining markets. For example, refer back to the depiction of the product market in figures 3.1–3.3 and consider the possibilities for the labor market. One possibility is that the real wage is above its equilibrium value resulting in an excess supply of labor. In this case, some workers are unemployed and therefore earn a lower level of income than originally planned. This leads the unemployed to restrict their purchases in the product market and implies that the effective demand for output is less than the notional demand. The demand for output is therefore overstated in figures 3.1–3.3. Now, suppose instead that the real wage is too low so that there is excess demand in the labor market. In this case, firms are unable to hire all the workers they desire and therefore cannot produce their planned level of output. Thus, the effective supply of output is less than its notional value and the supply of output is overstated in figures 3.1–3.3. In either case, at least one of the curves is mis-specified, rendering the subsequent analysis incorrect. This example clearly illustrates that the type of disequilibrium encountered in other markets has a direct bearing on the behavior of agents within a market. To understand how an economy behaves when nonmarket-clearing prices prevail, we must consider the situation in all markets at once. We need to make clear which agents are constrained in which markets and we must take these constraints into account when calculating supply and demand schedules. We now turn to a general equilibrium approach to show how to handle these matters in a rigorous fashion.

B. Fixed Prices in General Equilibrium

(i) Walrasian Equilibria

In this section, a simple three-good model is developed in order to illustrate the differences between a Walrasian equilibrium brought about by price adjustment and a non-Walrasian equilibrium generated by quantity adjustment with fixed prices. The three goods are a nonstorable consumption good, leisure, and money, with money held as a store of value. There are two types of economic agents: consumers and firms. Labor is the only productive input.[4]

I begin by describing the problems faced by consumers and firms when they believe that they will be able to purchase and sell all they desire in each market. With no fear of unemployment or shortages in the goods market, consumers choose consumption, leisure, and money holdings to maximize utility subject to a budget constraint. The only other constraint they face comes from the fact that they cannot work more than 24 hours in a day. Formally, let $U(c,1,\frac{m}{p})$ denote the consumer's utility function, with c representing consumption; 1, leisure; m, money holdings; and p, the price of the consumption good (so that $\frac{m}{p}$ represents real money balances). Utility is assumed to be increasing in each argument (money represents wealth and enters the utility function since it is used to finance future consumption). Then, letting w denote the wage and $\bar{m}$ denote initial money holdings, the consumer's daily problem is to choose c, 1, and $\frac{m}{p}$ to maximize:

(1) $U(c,1,\frac{m}{p})$ subject to: $cp + m = (24 - 1)w + \bar{m}$.

The budget constraint states that expenditures on consumption (cp) plus money holdings (m) must equal income [$(24-1)w$] plus initial money holdings. The solution to this problem yields a demand for consumption, a supply of labor, and a demand for money, all of which are functions of the price, wage, and initial money holdings - $c^{nd}(p,w,\bar{m})$, $L^{ns}(p,w,\bar{m})$ and $m^{nd}(p,w,\bar{m})$, respectively (L represents labor services and is therefore equal to $24-1$). In each case, the superscript n is used to remind the reader that these are the consumer's *notional* functions since they are derived under the assumption that the consumer is not rationed in any market. Note that consumption is a function of prices, *not* income, in this setting since leisure (and hence income) is a choice variable for the consumer.

To derive the *effective* demand curves, we would have to take into account any constraints the consumer might face in the marketplace. For example, if labor was in excess supply, the consumer might not be able to work more than, say, $\bar{L}$ hours per day. The constraint (24 – 1) $\leq \bar{L}$ would then have to be added to (1). If the consumer faced a constraint in the product market due to an insufficient supply of output, then a constraint such as $c \leq \bar{c}$ would have to be added to (1). These cases will be considered in detail below when I discuss the notion of a non-Walrasian equilibrium. It is important to note, however, that in each case, the effective demand and supply functions that result from (1) will be functions of these constraints as well as the price and wage levels.

Turn next to the firm's problem. Each firm's goal is to maximize profit. If there are no labor shortages or problems selling output, then the firm's objective is to choose labor (L) to maximize profit, or:

(2) $f(L)p - wL$.

In (2), $f(L)$ represents the production function. It is well known that profit is maximized by hiring labor until the marginal product of the last worker hired $(f'(L))$ equals the real wage. This condition yields a demand for labor and a supply of output that are functions of the real wage - $L^{nd}(\frac{w}{p})$ and $q^{ns}(\frac{w}{p})$, respectively (of course, $q^{ns} = f(L^{nd})$). Once again, the superscript n signifies that these are notional functions, since the firms face no market-imposed constraints. As with the consumer, effective demand and supply functions for the firm are derived by adding any product or labor market constraints to (2).

We are now in position to describe the traditional microeconomic notion of equilibrium.

Definition: For any given level of initial money holdings, a *Walrasian equilibrium* is a price and wage pair (p^*, w^*) such that $L^{ns}(p^*, w^*, \bar{m}) = L^{nd}(\frac{w^*}{p^*})$ and $c^{nd}(p^*, w^*, m) = q^{ns}(\frac{w^*}{p^*})$.

This definition states that a Walrasian equilibrium occurs when prices and wages equate notional supply and demand in each market. When such is the case, agents are justified in assuming that they will be able to carry out all their plans.

It is easy to think of examples in which, in reality, markets do not clear. Unemployment signifies excess supply in the labor market, waiting lists for foreign cars signify excess demand in some auto markets, and so on. Thus, it is clear that the economy is not always in a Walrasian equilibrium. We have tended to focus on this concept of equilibrium not because it describes reality but because we have believed that market forces always cause the economy to move towards a Walrasian equilibrium. If this is true, then this concept allows us to predict where the economy is headed. We have argued above, however, that it is not clear that the economy will indeed tend towards such a state. In addition, casual observation suggests that price and wage rigidities exist that often keep markets from clearing. It is therefore necessary to examine the behavior of the economy when non-Walrasian prices prevail.

(ii) Non-Walrasian Equilibria

Suppose that prices and wages are fixed in the short run at non-Walrasian levels due to unexplained rigidities. When the economy fails to achieve a Walrasian equilibrium, some agents will not be able to carry out all their planned transactions. Once this has been discovered, these agents will have to adjust accordingly. Such adjustments will, of course, alter the economywide supply and demand schedules in many markets. As long as supply and demand remain unequal, these adjustments will continue to be made. At some point, hopefully, supply and demand will balance. If they do, then the economy is said to have achieved a non-Walrasian equilibrium.

To gain some insight into the nature of a non-Walrasian equilibrium, an example is provided to show how such a state might be achieved. Suppose that the real wage and the price level are both above their market-clearing levels so that there is excess supply in both the labor and product markets. Excess supply in the labor market implies unemployment and a constraint on the number of hours each consumer can work. When (1) is resolved with this added constraint, an effective demand for output is obtained that depends on the tightness of this labor market constraint. For the firm, excess supply in the product market implies that they cannot sell all the output they had planned on producing. When (2) is resolved, taking into account this product market constraint, it yields an effective demand for labor that depends on the tightness of the sales constraint. Different constraints in the labor and product markets yield different levels of effective demand. If there exists a set of constraints such that the effective demand for labor by firms equals the supply of labor at the same time that the effective demand for output equals the supply, then the plans of consumers and producers formed by taking into account the market imposed constraints will be mutually consistent. If this state is ever achieved, the economy will be in a type of equilibrium, since (effective) supply and demand are equal and therefore all planned (albeit constrained) transactions can be carried out.

We are now in a position to formally define a non-Walrasian equilibrium. Let L_w and L_f denote the labor market constraints faced by workers and firms, respectively, and let $\bar{c}$ and $\bar{q}$ represent the product market constraints on purchases and sales, respectively.[5] Then a non-Walrasian equilibrium can be defined as follows.

Definition: For any given price/wage pair (p,w) and any initial level of money holdings, a *non-Walrasian equilibrium* is a set of constraints $(L_w^*, L_f^*, \bar{c}^*, \bar{q}^*)$ such that, when these constraints are taken into account by consumers and firms, effective demand and supply are equated in all markets.

We now turn to an explicit derivation of the non-Walrasian equilibria in order to compare them with the Walrasian equilibrium.

(iii) Properties of Non-Walrasian Equilibria

Whether workers or firms are constrained in a given market depends on the structure of prices and wages. For the model introduced above, there are four possibilities (see table 3.1). In the first case, workers are constrained in the labor market and the firm is constrained in the product market. This case occurs when the notional demand for labor falls short of the notional supply (so that there is unemployment) and the notional supply of output exceeds the notional demand (so that the firm cannot sell all its output). For reasons to be discussed below, this case is referred to as "Keynesian unemployment." The second possibility occurs when labor is constrained in both markets. Thus, not only are workers unemployed, but they also find it impossible to purchase the amount of the consumption good that they desire. This case is referred to as "classical unemployment." "Repressed inflation" occurs when there is excess demand in both markets. The final case, simply labeled X, occurs when the firm is constrained in both markets. The label "X" is used to signify that this type of non-Walrasian equilibrium cannot arise in our simple model.[6]

Table 3.1

	Labor market	Product market	Label
Which side of the market is constrained?	Labor	Firms	Keynesian unemployment
	Labor	Consumers	Classical unemployment
	Firms	Consumers	Repressed inflation
	Firms	Firms	X

Since different market constraints are imposed on the economy in each of the situations in table 3.1, the economy will adjust differently in each instance. To see how an equilibrium is achieved via quantity adjustments and to investigate the effectiveness of various government policies, I now turn to a detailed analysis of each case.

Keynesian Unemployment

Consider first the problem faced by workers. With the notional demand for labor falling short of supply, workers will not be able to work as many hours or earn as much income as they had planned. Instead, they will work as many hours as the market allows and then choose consumption and money holdings to maximize utility. Therefore, the effective supply of labor is exactly equal to the market constraint, L_w, and the worker's problem is to choose c and m to maximize:[7]

$$(3) \qquad U(c, 24-L_w, \frac{m}{p}) \qquad \text{subject to: } pc + m = (24 - L_w)w + \bar{m}.$$

Problem (3) is nothing more than (1) with the labor market constraint added. The solution to (3) yields an effective demand for consumption that depends only on the labor market constraint (remember that prices, wages and initial money holdings are assumed to be fixed).

The functional relationship between the effective demand for consumption and L_w has some interesting and familiar properties. To begin with, since income is equal to hours worked multiplied by the wage, and since the wage is fixed, once L_w is set by the market so is the worker's income. Changes in this labor market constraint result in movements in income, thereby triggering a change in consumption. Thus, consumption is simply a function of income which, in this case, is a parameter set by the market (as far as the worker is concerned). Turn next to the nature of the demand function. If we assume that present and future consumption are both normal goods and that the worker uses savings to finance consumption when it is impossible to find work, i.e., when $L_w = 0$, then this consumption function takes on the form depicted in figure 3.4 (the superscript e is used to denote an effective demand or supply curve so that c^{ed} represents the effective demand for consumption). All macroeconomists will immediately recognize this as nothing more than the Keynesian consumption function. It states that as the labor market constraint is relaxed (allowing the worker to work more hours), income and consumption both increase. However, since future consumption is a normal good, each extra dollar of income translates into less than one dollar's worth of extra consumption (the remainder goes into savings). Thus, the marginal propensity to consume, i.e., the slope of the consumption function, is less than unity.

Figure 3.4

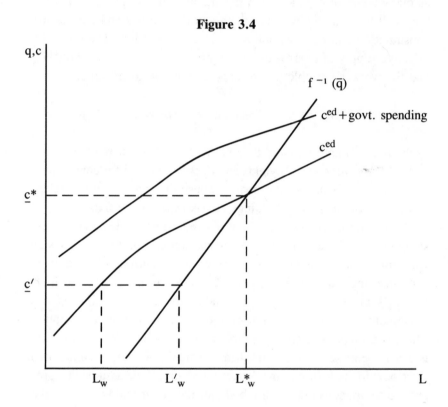

The solution to the firm's problem in the presence of Keynesian unemployment is easy to characterize. Since the firm cannot sell all it wants to, it will simply produce the level of output demanded. Thus, the effective supply of output is equal to the sales constraint, $\bar{q}$. The effective demand for labor is then equal to the number of workers needed to produce exactly $\bar{q}$ units of output. This value is given by the inverse of the production function evaluated at $\bar{q}$. As the sales constraint is relaxed (allowing the firm to sell more output), the effective demand for labor increases. This positively sloped function is also depicted in figure 3.4.

To derive the non-Walrasian equilibrium, consider an arbitrary labor market constraint such as L_w in figure 3.4. For this constraint to be part of a non-Walrasian equilibrium, there would have to be a corresponding product market constraint that leads to equality between effective demand and supply in all markets. From figure 3.4, the labor market constraint (L_w) translates into an effective demand for consumption of $\bar{c}'$. However, when firms face this constraint in the product market, they reveal an effective demand for labor of L'_w. Since, the effective demand for labor (L'_w) is greater than the effective supply (L_w), we conclude that L_w cannot be part of a non-Walrasian equilibrium. In fact, this sort of argument rules out all constraints except L^*_w and $\bar{c}^*$. It is easy to see these constraints *do* constitute a non-Walrasian equilibrium, since when the workers face L^*_w they reveal an effective demand for consumption of $\bar{c}^*$, and when the firms face a constraint of $\bar{c}^*$ in the product market, they will want to hire L^*_w workers.

This equilibrium is characterized by involuntary unemployment even though the actions of consumers and producers are mutually consistent. This follows from the fact that at the fixed wage and price levels the notional supply of labor exceeds demand.[8] Equilibrium is reached when the agents realize that they cannot carry out their notional plans and instead take into account the market-imposed constraints. Their final *constrained* desires are mutually consistent but, if it were possible, workers would prefer to work more hours and firms would prefer to sell more output. Finally, note that once this equilibrium is reached there are no longer any market signals present to put upward or downward pressure on wages and/or prices. Since firms are selling exactly what they produce and there are no unsatisfied customers demanding more output, there is no reason for the firm to raise or lower its price. Likewise, in the labor market workers are providing exactly the level of labor services demanded by employers, and thus there is no downward pressure on the real wage. *Quantity adjustments can remove the market signals that we usually assume will lead to price changes.*

Why is this case referred to as "Keynesian unemployment?" One rationale has already been offered: the effective demand for consumption closely mimics the traditional Keynesian consumption function. This, however, is not the primary reason for the nomenclature. Instead, this label refers to the types of policies that will be effective in lowering unemployment. The traditional Keynesian prescription for lowering unemployment is an increase in aggregate demand brought about by either an increase in government spending or a reduction in taxes. It is argued that unemployment stems from insufficient aggregate demand which keeps firms from expanding and increasing employment. On the other hand, the classical theory argues that unemployment stems from real wages that are too high. It is argued that by simply allowing the market to function unimpeded, real wages would fall and unemployment would disappear. An examination of these two policies in this setting reveals that only the former policy will work.

Consider first the Keynesian solution. An increase in aggregate demand (due to, say, an increase in government spending) stimulates the economy by relaxing the product market constraint faced by firms. As firms realize that they can sell more output, they respond by hiring more labor. This, in turn, increases consumer income and feeds back to the product market by further increasing aggregate demand (since consumption rises). The chain reaction continues, producing Keynesian multiplier-like effects, until a new non-Walrasian equilibrium is reached with lower unemployment and an increase in output that exceeds the increase in government spending. This can be seen clearly in figure 3.4, where the increase in government spending causes the aggregate demand curve (which is equal to the effective demand for consumption plus government spending) to shift upward and leads to a new equilibrium with higher employment, output, and consumption.

What would be the effect of lowering the real wage? The classical argument in favor of such a policy runs along the following lines. A fall in the real wage should trigger an increase in the quantity of labor demanded while reducing labor supply. If this occurs, then the level of excess supply in the labor market will be diminished and unemployment will be lowered. Unfortunately, a reduction in the real wage has virtually no effect when unemployment is of the Keynesian variety. To see this, simply note that in the presence of Keynesian unemployment, firms do not produce more output because they are constrained in the product market, i.e., they would not be able to sell the extra output.

Lowering the real wage will not relax this constraint and therefore it will not lead to an increase in labor demand. The fact that workers are constrained in the labor market implies that labor supply will not be affected either. Before the reduction in the real wage, workers are willing to work as many hours as the market allows and small changes in compensation will not change that. Therefore, policies aimed at lowering the real wage will not affect the unemployment rate.

Classical Unemployment

This case differs from Keynesian unemployment in only one respect: the situation in the product market. Under classical unemployment, firms are unconstrained and therefore able to operate on their notional supply and demand curves. Workers are constrained in both the product and labor markets; they work as much as the market allows and consume whatever firms choose to produce. Equilibrium employment (L^*) is therefore determined by evaluating the firm's notional demand for labor at the current real wage, i.e., $L^* = L^{nd}(\frac{W}{P})$. Equilibrium output corresponds to a point on the firm's notional supply of output, i.e., $q^{ns}=f(L^*)$.

Since firms are unconstrained in the product market, a reduction in the real wage will be an effective way to combat unemployment. Profit maximization dictates that unconstrained firms should hire workers until the marginal product of the last worker hired equals the real wage. As the real wage falls, firms will respond by increasing employment.

In contrast, the Keynesian remedy for unemployment, an increase in aggregate demand, will have no effect on employment. Firms are already producing and selling all they desire. The increase in government spending will not alter the profit-maximizing level of output (with price fixed, marginal product still equals the real wage at the original level of employment), it will simply crowd out private consumption.

A comparison of Keynesian and classical unemployment reveals that it is the type of disequilibrium encountered in the product market that determines the effectiveness of various government policies. If there is excess demand (in the notionals) so that workers are constrained in consumption, then the only effective way to reduce unemployment is by somehow lowering the real wage. When firms face sales constraints, then the Keynesian solution of aggregate demand management is most effective and policies aimed at lowering real wages have no employment effect. This difference follows from the fact that non-Walrasian prices create links across markets that are not present otherwise. For example, when price is high enough to produce excess supply in the product market, the tightness of the sales constraint directly determines the level of employment (since firms hire only enough workers to produce whatever is demanded). An increase in the demand for output loosens this constraint, causing firms to expand their labor forces. A qualitatively different link exists when the product market is characterized by excess demand. In that case, firms can sell their profit-maximizing level of output; thus, employment is determined by the equation equating marginal product and the real wage. Only a reduction in the real wage can reduce unemployment. This contrast should make it clear how important the links between markets can be in the presence of nonmarket-clearing prices.

Repressed Inflation

Repressed inflation occurs when there is excess demand in both markets. The label refers to the fact that increases in price and the real wage are required to equate notional supply and demand in each market. As in the other cases, however, if prices are not flexible, quantity adjustments will result in a non-Walrasian equilibrium.

Consumers/workers are constrained only in the product market, unable to reach their desired level of consumption. In response to this constraint, they simply consume as much as the market allows ($\bar{c}$) and then choose leisure to maximize utility. Formally, the worker's problem is to maximize:

(4) $U(\bar{c}, 24 - L, \frac{m}{p})$ subject to: $p\bar{c} + m = (24 - L)w + \bar{m}$.

Problem (4) is equivalent to the (1) with the product market constraint added and the solution yields an effective supply of labor that is a function of the tightness of the consumption constraint. As this constraint is relaxed, thereby allowing the worker to purchase more output, the consumer responds by working more hours. This positive relationship is depicted in figure 3.5 as the effective labor supply curve.[9]

Figure 3.5

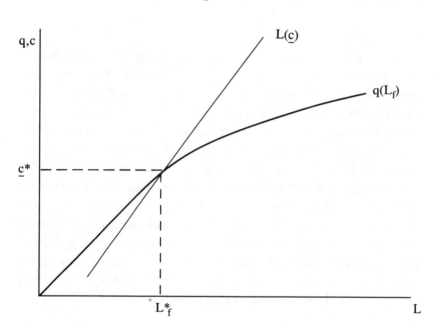

Under repressed inflation the firm is unable to reach its optimal employment level. Constrained profits are therefore maximized by hiring as much labor as possible and using it to produce as much output as the technology allows. Any increase in labor supply will be welcome, resulting in an increase in economic activity. This positive relationship is represented in figure 3.5 by the upward sloping effective supply of output (as a function of L_f, the firm's labor market constraint).

The non-Walrasian equilibrium is characterized by a balance between effective supply and demand in each market. An analysis similar to that used in the case of Keynesian unemployment reveals that this occurs at the intersection of the two curves in figure 3.5. Since there is no unemployment in this regime, no detailed analysis of the equilibrium or policy effectiveness is offered in this monograph. Interested readers are referred to Benassy (1982) or Malinvaud (1977) for a discussion of these issues.

X

The final possibility listed in table 3.1, labeled X, occurs when the firm is constrained in both markets. Under our assumption that the consumption good is nonstorable, no non-Walrasian equilibrium with this characteristic exists. The reason for this is simple. If the firm is constrained in the product market, unable to sell what it desires to produce, and if inventories cannot be carried into the next period, why would the firm ever want to increase employment? An increase in employment would only result in greater production. If the firm is unable to sell or store additional output, then the increase in employment would obviously lower profits (by increasing costs without changing revenue). If the model is extended to allow for a durable consumption good, then this regime emerges as a possibility. However, since this case would not entail unemployment, I will simply refer interested readers to Benassy (1982) for a discussion of the extended model.

If we place fairly mild restrictions on the utility and production functions in the model above, then it can be shown that for any price/wage pair there is a unique equilibrium. Whether the equilibrium is characterized by Keynesian unemployment, classical unemployment, repressed inflation, or a Walrasian equilibrium depends on the structure of wages and prices. With specific functional forms for $U(\ )$ and $f(\ )$ we could derive the conditions under which each regime applies. Figure 3.6 gives us some idea as to what those conditions will look like, with (p^*, w^*) representing the unique Walrasian equilibrium price vector. This is the only price vector that equates notional supply and demand in all markets.

A lower price level generates excess supply in the product market and, if it is accompanied by a lower real wage, repressed inflation results. All remaining price/wage combinations generate some level of equilibrium unemployment. When the price level is high, there will be excess supply in the product market and unemployment will be of the Keynesian variety. Low prices generate excess demand in the product market, thereby producing classical unemployment. The boundaries between the regions depend on the nature of the utility and production functions, but the qualitative properties of figure 3.6 are fairly robust.

Figure 3.6

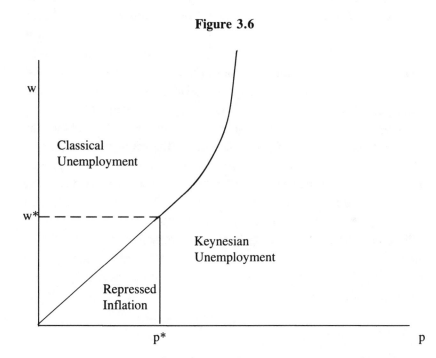

At this point it is useful to step back and summarize the basic insights provided this fixed price model. First, we have seen that quantity adjustments in the presence of fixed, non-Walrasian prices can produce an equilibrium in which constrained supply and demand schedules are equated. Once this equilibrium is reached, all market forces that might be expected to cause prices and/or wages to change disappear. Therefore, if, for some reason, non-Walrasian prices prevail and quantities adjust to clear markets, it is conceivable that the economy will remain at an equilibrium characterized by less than full employment. In other words, the economy might not (and probably would not) gravitate naturally towards the full employment Walrasian equilibrium.

Second, non-Walrasian prices create links across markets that influence the types of policies that will be effective. Furthermore, the links can produce Keynesian features such as multiplier effects and a traditional Keynesian consumption function. This follows from the fact that constraints faced by agents in one market directly influence their behavior in other markets. For example, as the sales constraint faced by firms in the product market is relaxed, they respond by increasing their demand for labor. These links have been referred to as "spillover effects" in the literature and their importance is evident if one simply compares the cases titled Keynesian and classical unemployment. In each case, the labor market is characterized by excess supply but the policies that will be effective in reducing unemployment differ across regimes. Keynesian unemployment occurs when firms are constrained in the product market and policies that loosen this constraint lower unemployment (such as an increase in government spending or lower taxes). Classical unemployment occurs when the firm is totally unconstrained. This implies that unemployment can only be reduced by moving the firm down its labor demand schedule (by lowering the real wage). Thus, the type of notional disequilibrium encountered in the product market determines the appropriate policy.

(iv) Other Insights

The simple model presented above is representative of the first models used to illustrate the importance of non-Walrasian equilibria. A great deal of subsequent work retained many of the features of this model but extended it in a manner that would allow investigation of much broader issues. For example, Barro and Grossman (1976) added a much more elaborate monetary sector (including financial assets and capital) and grafted on a dynamic process to explain changes in prices and wages in order to examine the relationship between inflation and unemployment in a disequilibrium model. Their set-up also allowed them to investigate the importance of inflationary expectations and the efficacy of monetary policy. Obst (1978) also focused on the role of monetary policy in the disequilibrium framework by investigating the impact of a policy rule that keeps the money supply growing at a constant rate. He demonstrated that due to monetary factors, such a rule would create a trade cycle and keep the economy from converging to a steady-state equilibrium. Dixit and Norman (1980), among others, used a simple disequilibrium model to investigate the implications of sticky prices for trade issues such as the effect of devaluation on the balance of payments.

Additional theoretical insights have been obtained by examining more explicitly dynamic versions of the simple model. In a multi-period model, Neary and Stiglitz (1983) demonstrated that even when current prices are correct (in the sense that they are at the Walrasian values) non-Walrasian equilibria may arise instead due to changes in behavior caused by expectations about future prices (and, therefore, future market constraints). In other words, a Walrasian outcome requires that present prices equal their market-clearing values *and* that all agents expect *all future prices* to be at their Walrasian levels as well.

There has been a great deal of empirical work using the simple fixed-price framework as well. Methods for estimating disequilibrium models have been developed and Quandt (1978), among others, has found ways of testing whether the data conform better to an equilibrium or a disequilibrium model. (For an excellent survey of some of the issues involved, see Quandt and Rosen 1988.) In addition, surveys have been conducted in which firms were asked about their perceived market constraints. The answers to the survey questions allow one to obtain estimates of how much of current unemployment is of the Keynesian variety (as opposed to classical unemployment). It is also possible to use the data to infer the impact of government policy on the type of unemployment experienced over time. For a survey of the work in this area, interested readers are referred to Laffont (1985).

C. Endogenous Pricing

Although the early fixed-price literature clearly provided many valuable insights, it cannot be considered a complete theory since it provided no explanation of how prices are determined. There have been a number of recent attempts to rectify this shortcoming. The purpose of this section is to provide a cursory historical review of some of the more notable attempts and the insights they have yielded.

(i) First Attempts

Benassy's 1976 article appears to have been the first to address the issue of endogenous pricing in a disequilibrium framework. In Benassy's model, firms announce their prices at the beginning of each period and then quantities adjust to clear markets. Consumers are allowed to send signals to producers in order to provide them with some feeling as to the level of excess demand inherent in the market (these signals are in the form of *desired*, as opposed to *actual*, transactions). Firms then use these signals to adjust their prices. An equilibrium occurs when firms arrive at a price vector that remains stable across periods. The main goal of the article was to determine whether equilibrium could occur at non-Walrasian prices and, in fact, Benassy was able to prove the existence of a non-Walrasian equilibrium price vector. There are, however, several problems with this approach. First, it is not clear that the signals sent by consumers are adequate measures of disequilibrium and it is unclear why firms should rely on such a measure in setting prices. Second, by assuming that prices must remain fixed in the short run, Benassy rules out the interesting (and plausible) possibility that firms may attempt to alter their market-imposed constraints by changing their prices. Finally, this model simply assumes that prices adjust more slowly than quantities without providing an explanation as to why this should be so.

The Benassy paper was significant since it represented the first attempt to endogenize the price decision while, at the same time, allowing firms to take into account market-imposed constraints. I also believe that it was significant because it marked the end of the line for strict fixed-price models. Benassy retained the assumption that in the very short run prices could not adjust and therefore ruled out the possibility that agents might attempt to loosen market constraints by altering the terms of trade. However, in reality, firms unable to sell all their output often attempt to increase sales by lowering their price. Likewise, by reducing their wage demands, jobless workers might increase their likelihood of employment. It therefore seems more reasonable to assume that market constraints are in the form of schedules that tell agents what transactions can be made at various prices. For sales-constrained firms, the schedule would tell the firm how much it could expect to sell as a function of its price. By extending fixed-price models to allow for constraint schedules, it becomes possible to investigate models in which price and quantity decisions are made jointly. In doing so, the strict adherence to price or quantity adjustments to clear markets is abandoned.

The first papers to adopt this alternative approach were written in the late 1970s by Frank Hahn (see Hahn 1977a, 1977b, 1978). Hahn assumed that each rationed agent would form some sort of conjecture as to how the market-imposed constraints were related to his/her price offers. Agents would then choose price and quantity offers to maximize utility with these constraints in mind. The main goal of this research project was to investigate whether non-Walrasian equilibria would exist in such a setting. The answer to this question depends on the type of conjectures allowed. It seems obvious that one would want to apply some sort of notion of rationality when restricting conjectures, and that is exactly what Hahn attempted to do. The first rationality condition used requires the conjectured and actual constraints to coincide at equilibrium. This simply implies that given the set of equilibrium transactions, conjectured and actual prices are equal. The second condition imposed is a type of "local rationality" requirement in that it states that in the neighborhood of equilibrium, the conjectured relationship between prices and trades must mimic the actual relationship. This is equivalent to requiring the slopes of the conjectured and actual constraint schedules to be equal when evaluated at equilibrium. With these two restrictions, Hahn proved that there exists at least one equilibrium characterized by non-Walrasian prices. The problem with this approach rests with the definition of a rational conjecture. As Hahn points out, his definition of rationality simply requires agents' guesses to be correct up to the level of first derivatives. Conjectures about higher order derivatives are still allowed to be arbitrary. Forcing agents to be globally correct in their conjectures seemed too strict to Hahn and too closely related to theories of imperfect competition (since such a requirement rules out the possibility of a Walrasian equilibrium). He refused to allow his theory of unemployment to rest on an inherent assumption of imperfect competition and was therefore unable to carry his work much further.

(ii) Imperfect Competition and Coordination Failures

When agents face constraints resulting from non-Walrasian prices, they must immediately abandon the perfectly competitive assumption that they can trade all they want to at the current price level. This leads one to think that theories of imperfect competition might provide the appropriate framework for the study of non-Walrasian economies. Oliver Hart, in his influential 1982 paper, "A Model of Imperfect Competition with Keynesian Features," was the first to apply this concept in a rigorous fashion. The major substantive difference between Hart's approach and Hahn's lies in Hart's assumption that agents correctly perceive the constraint schedules they face. This provides a general equilibrium model very much in the spirit of Chamberlain's theory of monopolistic competition. Firms, knowing the demand schedules they face, choose prices to maximize profits, and unionized labor, knowing the demand for labor schedule, chooses the wage rate to maximize utility. Equilibrium occurs when prices and wages are chosen to maximize the appropriate objective functions and all markets clear.

This abstract general equilibrium model is too complex to handle without placing restrictions on the utility and production functions. Therefore, Hart chose to work out an example in order to gain some insight into the nature of equilibrium. This was accomplished by placing enough restrictions on demand to guarantee the existence of equilibrium.[10] This equilibrium is characterized by *non-Walrasian* prices, suggesting that an unaided market economy will *not* tend to gravitate towards Walrasian, market-clearing prices. In other words, the selfish pursuit of private gain will not produce an efficient outcome.

A comparison between Hart's equilibrium and the Walrasian outcome reveals some interesting features. To begin with, in Hart's model, equilibrium employment is below and output prices are above the values that would be achieved in a perfectly competitive Walrasian economy. This implies that the non-Walrasian equilibrium generates unemployment of the Keynesian variety and that prices associated with classical unemployment or repressed inflation cannot emerge in equilibrium when prices are set optimally.[11] Furthermore, the Keynesian nature of equilibrium means that aggressive aggregate demand management is required to increase employment and aggregate income.[12] Finally, Hart also demonstrates that, as in the Keynesian unemployment case above, changes in government spending produce Keynesian multiplier-like effects in his model.

The Hart article proves that when rational, fully informed agents set prices to maximize utility (or profit), the economy may not end up in the Walrasian equilibrium. In fact, the resulting equilibrium will likely be troubled by underemployment that can only be reduced by Keynesian methods. One issue not addressed by Hart is whether or not this equilibrium is unique. This issue was avoided by choosing restrictions on the utility and production functions that guaranteed uniqueness. Subsequent work by a number of authors, most notably Heller (1986), indicates that, in general, imperfectly competitive behavior may produce several equilibria, all of which can be Pareto-ranked.[13]

The Heller model consists of two monopolistically competitive product markets and a perfectly competitive labor market. Therefore, except for the modeling of the labor market, the setting is equivalent to Hart's. To capture the notion that individuals tend to specialize in production but diversify in consumption, Heller assumes that income earned by workers in one sector is spent entirely on the output produced in the remaining sector. This assumption creates a vital link across sectors, since it implies that an increase in employment in one sector stimulates activity in the other sector by increasing demand.

The point of the Heller article is to demonstrate that such a model may possess multiple inefficient equilibria and that these equilibria can be Pareto-ranked. The intuition for these results is as follows. Consider the position of a typical sector-one firm in equilibrium. If this firm were to increase employment (in order to produce more output) there would be a spillover effect on sector two in that the increase in sector-one income would cause the demand for sector-two output to rise. In response to this increase in demand, sector-two firms would increase employment and (perhaps) raise prices. The increased activity in sector two then feeds back to sector one as sector-two income rises, and so on. In the end, income and demand will increase in both sectors, but, since the original situation was an equilibrium, the total increase in sector-one demand cannot be large enough to justify the initial increase in employment. Even though everyone except the original firm would benefit, the increase in employment would not occur. The problem is that each firm *alone* has such a small impact on aggregate income that it cannot cause a chain reaction of sufficient magnitude to justify increasing production. If, on the other hand, all firms were to *simultaneously* increase employment, the resulting increase in income could be large enough to make the increases in output profitable. Therefore, another equilibrium characterized by greater output, employment, and income might exist. Reaching this equilibrium, however, requires all firms to coordinate their production plans. The failure of the economy to reach the best equilibrium has therefore been labeled a "coordination failure."

The conclusion that coordination failures may generate multiple inefficient equilibria is reminiscent of Peter Diamond's result that when search is required to find employment, feedback mechanisms are created that can produce more than one equilibrium (see chapter 2 for details). In addition, in both cases the equilibria can be Pareto-ranked so that there is a role for government policy aimed at guiding the economy toward the best equilibrium. The fact that these seemingly unrelated models produce qualitatively similar results has not gone unnoticed.

In a recent paper, Cooper and John (1988) developed a simple abstract game theoretic model in an attempt to isolate the common forces at work. In their model, agents choose strategies in order to maximize their own payoff. These strategies may also affect the payoffs of other agents in the economy. For example, in the Hart/Heller framework, each firm's strategy consists of an output price and a level of employment. By changing employment, a firm in sector one can alter worker income, and hence demand in sector two. Consequently, strategy choices by sector-one firms affect the profits earned by sector-two firms and vice versa. In a search model, the worker's strategy would either be a level of search intensity or a reservation wage. In either case, changes in the strategy affect the likelihood that other workers find employment and the probability that firms fill vacancies.

Cooper and John's goal is to identify conditions under which (1) their model can support more than one equilibrium, (2) the equilibria are inefficient, and (3) the equilibria can be Pareto-ranked. They refer to these properties as "Keynesian features" since they are consistent with the Keynesian notion that an unaided economy can get stuck in an inefficient equilibrium at less than full employment. In order to describe their findings, I will make use of the following definitions.

Definition: An economy exhibits *positive spillovers* if an increase in one agent's strategy increases the payoff to all other agents. An economy exhibits *strategic complementarity* if an increase in one agent's strategy results in an increase in each remaining agent's optimal strategy.

Cooper and John prove that strategic complementarity is necessary for multiple equilibria and that positive spillovers lead to inefficiency. In addition, if positive spillovers are present, the equilibria can be Pareto-ranked with those characterized by more activity preferred. Consider the latter results first. Intuitively, positive spillovers are nothing more than positive externalities. Their existence implies that equilibrium will be inefficient, with agents choosing strategies below their optimal values. A small increase in each agent's strategy would increase economic activity and enhance social welfare. Positive spillovers are present in

Heller's model of imperfect competition, since an increase in sector-one employment leads to increased demand (and hence profits) in sector two. Note also that strategic complementarity is present since it is optimal for sector-two firms to respond to the increased demand by hiring extra labor and producing more output. The existence of positive externalities in Diamond's search model has already been established in chapter 2.

Now consider Cooper and John's first result. Equilibrium occurs when each agent, taking the strategies of all other agents as given, chooses an optimal strategy and the plans of all agents are mutually consistent. According to Cooper and John, if the economy is in an equilibrium and strategic complementarities are present, then a simultaneous increase in the strategies of all agents may lead to a new equilibrium. Furthermore, if strategic complementarities are not present, then there is at most one equilibrium.

The reason for this can be made clear by examining an example in detail. As noted above, Heller's imperfectly competitive economy exhibits strategic complementarity. Suppose that the economy is currently at rest in an equilibrium. Suppose further that all firms but one suddenly decide to increase output. As we have already seen, the increased activity by other firms results in an increase in the demand for the remaining firm's output. Thus, the optimal response is for the last firm to increase output as well (this is nothing more than strategic complementarity at work). In fact, by a similar argument, the increases in output by all other firms may also be optimal. A new equilibrium in which each firm produces more output may therefore exist.

What would have happened had strategic complementarities not been present? In such a case, an increase in every other firm's strategy (i.e., output) would actually discourage increased activity by the remaining firm. Thus, if all firms but one were to increase output, the optimal response by the last firm would be to decrease output—a simultaneous increase in output by all firms could not produce a new equilibrium. Intuitively, when the economy exhibits strategic complementarity, the increases in strategy choices reinforce each other, justifying the increased economic activity.

In summary, by building upon the insights provided by the early fixed-price literature, the literature on endogenous pricing has led to several important results. First, when price-setting agents take market-imposed constraints into account in calculating their optimal strategies, equilibrium will occur at *non-Walrasian* prices. In addition, equilibrium will be inefficient, with less employment and output than what would be predicted by a traditional Walrasian model. Furthermore, unemployment is of the Keynesian variety, implying that an increase in government spending or a decrease in taxes is required to stimulate the economy. Finally, more than one equilibrium may exist so that active government policy may be required to guide the economy to the best equilibrium.

A theme common to both the search literature and the literature on non-Walrasian equilibria is that small changes in the assumptions of the traditional Walrasian general equilibrium model may produce models that possess "Keynesian features"—multiple inefficient equilibria that can be Pareto-ranked. The work of Cooper and John clearly identifies the characteristics necessary for such a result: positive externalities must be present and an increase in economic activity by one agent must encourage other agents to increase their activity as well. Search and imperfectly competitive models are just two examples of economies possessing these properties.

D. Policy Implications

Policy analysis in a fixed-price framework is considerably more straightforward than it is in the presence of frictional, i.e., search-generated unemployment. This follows from the fact that the efficient level of unemployment in a fixed-price model is zero, since a social planner can always adjust prices so that markets clear. This would result in the competitive outcome and an efficient allocation of resources. Consequently, employment and welfare are perfectly correlated.

The goal of full employment can be achieved by allowing prices to adjust to their market-clearing levels or by removing, if possible, the factors that lead to price rigidities in the first place. However, assuming that such prescriptions are not feasible (as is likely to be the case), the appropriate corrective policy depends on the constraints faced by economic agents. In general, policies that relax these constraints are welfare-improving.

Essentially, all that can be said concerning policy follows from the insights discussed in sections B and C above. For example, we have already seen that in the case of Keynesian unemployment, fiscal policy aimed at increasing aggregate demand will stimulate the economy, increase the demand for labor, and reduce unemployment. It follows that: increased government spending; a reduction in income taxes; unemployment benefits, which increase the income of the jobless; wage subsidies, which increase the income of the employed; redistribution programs that transfer income from the wealthy to the poor (assuming that the poor save less than the rich); or other government programs that result in an increase in the aggregate demand for consumption goods will be effective ways to increase employment and welfare. Although superior policies always exist, minimum wages might even be welfare-improving if it could be demonstrated that the increase in the income of the employed (due to the increased wage) would more than compensate for the reduction in demand brought about by the unemployment created. On the other hand, these policies will have no impact on employment whatsoever if unemployment is of the classical variety. In such a situation, only policies that reduce the real wage will relax the constraints faced by the workers and expand output and employment.

As far as policy is concerned, the endogenous pricing models surveyed in section C provide two valuable insights. First, they imply that when profit- and utility-maximizing agents set prices and wages in an optimal manner taking market-imposed constraints into account, the result will be Keynesian unemployment. Therefore, unemployment due to monopoly power should be handled with old-fashioned Keynesian remedies. Second, as demonstrated by Heller (1986) and Cooper and John (1988), imperfectly competitive behavior can lead to coordination failures— the economy can get stuck in an equilibrium that is Pareto-dominated by another feasible equilibrium. This result, which is qualitatively identical to results obtained in the search literature, indicates that the government should play an active role in guiding the economy towards the best equilibrium. This provides further support for "pump-priming" and propaganda aimed at raising expectations about future economic prospects.

NOTES

1. By "true microeconomic principles" I mean utility and profit-maximizing behavior on the part of economic agents. Therefore, the "neoclassical synthesis" that produced IS-LM analysis would not qualify.

2. Patinkin (1956) was actually the first to address these issues. However, his interpretation of Keynes was, for the most part, ignored until Clower's work appeared.

3. Examples of recent attempts include Fisher (1972) and Eden (1981).

4. The analysis that follows draws heavily from the work of Barro and Grossman (1971), Malinvaud (1977), and Benassy (1982).

5. Of course, all of these constraints cannot be binding simultaneously. The case in which agents are not rationed in a particular market is handled by setting the appropriate constraint equal to infinity.

6. This nomenclature is attributed to Malinvaud (1977).

7. There are two well-known methods for calculating effective demand and supply schedules. In one method, due to Drèze (1975), agents take all market-imposed constraints into account simultaneously in formulating their plans. Alternatively, Benassy (1975, 1976) assumes that in determining the effective demand for a particular product, each agent takes into account all constraints faced in other markets but ignores the constraint faced in the market for the good in question. This distinction is not important for my purposes and thus, for simplicity, I will adopt the Drèze approach. For a detailed discussion of this point see Drazen (1980).

8. Since the excess supply is not actually observable in equilibrium (only effective demand is revealed in the market) some authors refer to this situation as "underemployment" as opposed to unemployment. I believe that they are probably correct, but I will choose not to push this distinction in this chapter. This point is discussed in greater detail in chapter 6.

9. The graphical representations of Keynesian unemployment and repressed inflation are due to Barro and Grossman (1971).

10. Existence of equilibrium in models of monopolistic competition can often be a serious problem. See Roberts and Sonnenschein (1976, 1977) for details.

11. The imperfectly competitive framework provides firms with market power that they exploit, resulting in excessively high output prices. These high prices generate excess supply in product market notionals, and hence, Keynesian unemployment.

12. Interestingly, some empirical support can be found for the result that most unemployment is of the Keynesian variety. In recent papers Bouissou, Laffont, and Vuong (1983) and Artus, Laroque, and Michel (1982) report on survey data collected in an attempt to determine whether the unemployment experienced in Europe during the 1970s was of the Keynesian or classical variety. The authors concluded that over 60 percent of the unemployment was Keynesian (in that firms viewed themselves as constrained in a manner consistent with Keynesian unemployment) while less than one-quarter could be classified as classical unemployment (see the conclusion for details).

13. See also Kiyotaki (1985), Roberts (1987), and Weitzman (1982).

4
Implicit Contracts

One of the lessons of the recent articles on trade frictions and the emerging literature on coordination failures is that economies can exhibit Keynesian features (e.g., multiple underemployment equilibria, multipliers) even if wages and prices are perfectly flexible. Nevertheless, wage rigidity remains an important element in much current macroeconomic analysis. Perhaps this is because many believe that to truly understand unemployment we must first determine why wages do not fall when unemployment persists; or perhaps it is because many are convinced that wage rigidity is a real phenomenon that needs to be explained.[1] In any event, much recent work has been focused on providing an explanation of wage rigidity in an environment in which rational utility-maximizing agents operate. Implicit in much of this work is the assumption that if we can explain wage rigidity, a theory of unemployment will follow naturally.

The theory of implicit contracts (e.g., Bailey 1974 and Azariadis 1975) represents one of the first successful attempts to provide a microeconomic model in which wage rigidity arises as an optimal equilibrium phenomenon. This literature differs from standard neoclassical microeconomics in that it does *not* assume that the primary role of the wage rate is to clear the labor market. Instead, wages are viewed as the outcome of a complex process (that may or may not involve negotiations) in which the firm and its employees manage to decide how to split the rents that are generated by employment. Jobs are viewed as *long-term* attachments so that if, at the time of initial contact between the firm and its employee, the future state of the economy is uncertain, the wage pattern will reflect the relative attitudes towards risk of the contracting parties. Assuming that workers are risk averse and that firms are risk neutral, it can be shown that, in some cases, the optimal contract is characterized by future wages that are independent of the state of the economic environment. That is, wage rigidity is efficient. Unfortunately, efficient contracts generally do not involve layoffs during economic slumps and therefore, even though wage rigidity can be explained, the link between wage rigidity and unemployment is lost.

The purpose of this chapter is to review the literature on labor contracts while paying particular attention to its ability to explain unemployment.[2] We begin in section A by briefly outlining the basic assumptions underlying the early work in this area. Included are the suppositions that the terms of the contract are (at least in part) isolated from market forces, and that workers are more risk averse than firms. We then demonstrate how these assumptions can create an environment in which wage rigidity can be expected to emerge in equilibrium.

The weaknesses of this approach are highlighted in the third portion of section A. There are at least two major shortcomings. First, as noted above, the theory cannot account for layoff unemployment. Intuitively, in an efficient contract, the risk-neutral firm provides insurance to its risk-averse employees by paying the same wage rate regardless of whether it is facing good or bad times. The firm is willing to bear all the risk since by doing so it can reduce its expected wage bill. However, a similar argument implies that workers should also desire to insure against perverse economic states in other dimensions as well. For example, workers should request (and firms should be willing to grant) work-sharing arrangements that reduce the variability in leisure hours across future states; layoffs are rarely optimal. Moreover, even when layoffs are optimal it can be shown that contracts actually reduce the number of layoffs below what would occur in an economy in which labor is traded on a spot market.

The second deficiency concerns the implementation of these *implicit* contracts. Although it is argued that no formal contract is necessary, these implicit agreements are treated as if they are binding. This may be problematic. After all, for the wage to be fixed at a level that allows the firm to at least break even (in expected value terms), workers must earn more than their marginal product in bad times and less than their marginal product in good times. However, if this is the case, what would prevent a worker from quitting during good times and seeking a higher wage on the spot market?

Subsequent work aimed at circumventing these problems is reviewed in section B. To deal with the implementation problem, efficient contracts are required to satisfy additional constraints designed to guarantee that it is in the interest of both parties to continue the employment relationship in all economic states. This alters the properties of the efficient contracts. Most notably, it results in contracts in which wages are rigid downward but not upward, i.e., wages rise as the firm's economic condition improves, but they do not fall during economic downturns.

The first problem, explaining unemployment, is somewhat more difficult to handle. Most of the work aimed at solving this problem modifies the basic model by assuming that the firm and its workers possess different amounts of information about the economic environment. For example, the actual marginal product of labor might be known only by the firm. In such situations, the terms of the contract must be altered in one of two ways. First, since the uninformed party might not trust the informed party to accurately reveal what they know, the contract could be written so that wage payments and employment do not depend on the private information. Alternatively, the contract could be structured so that it is in the interest of the informed party to correctly reveal the relevant information. This would allow the terms of the contract to be conditioned on the state of the economy and allow more flexibility than the first approach. Of course, in order to elicit the appropriate information, the proper incentives must be built into the contract. This naturally changes the character of the optimal contract and, under certain conditions, can lead to underemployment. Unfortunately, the conditions required to produce underemployment are either contradicted by empirical findings or inconsistent with the conditions necessary to generate wage rigidity. The conclusion is that contract theory has not yet been able to develop a theory of unemployment based on a microeconomic rationale for wage rigidity.

Some brief concluding remarks concerning the future role of this literature are offered in section C.

A. The Basic Model

(i) Setting the Stage

In a frictionless, perfectly competitive economy there is no reason for a worker to feel any particular attachment to a firm. If the firm's current wage offer were to fall below the market wage, all workers would quit and seek employment elsewhere. This is, of course, one of the reasons that all firms choose to offer the market-determined wage rate. In a more realistic model, with labor market frictions and/or firm-specific human capital, this knife-edge result disappears and the market's ability to dictate the terms at which labor services are exchanged is considerably weakened. In the former case, quitting is costly to both the worker and the firm since it takes time and effort to find a new job or fill the newly created vacancy. In the latter case, the current employer values the worker's services more than any other firm, since the worker has already been trained and has acquired the necessary productivity-enhancing human capital. To replace the worker would be costly to the firm (since it would have to train a new employee), and by quitting the worker would be moving to a new job in which he or she is, at least at first, less productive. In either setting, the worker-firm relationship is insulated from market forces and some other method must be used to determine how to split the rents produced by employment. In addition, once the split has been determined, both the worker and the firm will have an interest in maintaining the relationship on a long-term basis. This follows from the fact that frictions produce an environment in which the value of a current job exceeds the sum of what the two parties could earn in their next best alternatives.

The assumption that there is a long-term relationship between the firm and its employees that is at least somewhat immune to market forces is supported by recent empirical findings. As Sherwin Rosen (1985) notes (the references have been updated as necessary):

> Many features of labor markets bear little resemblance to impersonal Walrasian auction markets. Chief among them is the remarkable degree of observed worker-firm attachment. Martin Feldstein's (1975) surprising finding that over 70

percent of layoffs are temporary with most laid-off workers ultimately returning to their original employers, was confirmed on similar aggregate data by David Lilien (1980) and by much different methods on micro-panel data in a recent study by Lawrence Katz (1986c). The typical adult male worker spends twenty years or more on a single job (Hall 1982) and the probability of job turnover is a sharply declining function of job tenure (e.g., Mincer and Jovanovic 1981; Randolph 1983). Most job changes in a worker's life occur at younger ages, and a person who has persisted in the same job for a few years is likely to continue employment in it for a long time to come. If tenure is de jure in academia, it is de facto in much of the labor market at large (p. 1147).

Taking as given this long-term attachment, the contract literature assumes that workers and firms bargain over wages and employment at the time of initial contact.[3] The outside market serves as a check on the market power of both sides, since, if either side attempts to secure a contract that is too unfavorable to the other side, the other side will sever the relationship. However, as we have argued above, in the presence of trading frictions the market will provide only a small check and much will be left to negotiate over. Throughout this literature, the actual bargaining process is not modeled and no attempt is made to predict the exact outcome of the negotiations. Instead, it is assumed that the outcome will be efficient (in the sense that to make one party better off, the remaining party must be harmed) and the properties shared by all efficient contracts are derived.

At the time that the terms of the contract are determined, there are likely to be many aspects about the future that are uncertain. For example, technology and consumer tastes cannot be predicted with perfect accuracy. Since the firm's demand for labor fluctuates with these factors, there may be a desire to write contracts that make future employment and compensation a function of the future economic environment. This is feasible only if the variables in question are observable, e.g., changes in price may reflect changes in tastes. Whether or not it is desirable depends on the contracting parties' attitudes towards risk. Of course, if workers had easy access to capital markets, they could purchase insurance against fluctuations in income and employment elsewhere and labor contracts would be redundant. However, such insurance is generally not available and, since the terms of the contract determine the amount of uncertainty faced by each party, the assumptions made concerning attitudes towards risk are vital to the analysis.

The early work in this area made what seems to be the most natural assumption—workers are assumed to be risk averse while firms are risk neutral. The idea underlying this assumption is that all agents are basically risk averse (at least to some degree), but since firms are generally owned by shareholders who hold diversified portfolios, the firm's owners need not worry much about firm-specific risk. On the other hand, wages are the primary source of income for most workers and, as noted above, it is virtually impossible to purchase private insurance against changes in employment status. Therefore, firms and workers differ in their ability to shift firm-specific risk. This results in an environment in which firms act as if they are risk neutral while workers are risk averse.

To summarize, the contract literature assumes that, for some reason, a risk-neutral firm operating in an uncertain environment is momentarily tied to its risk-averse employees. These parties attempt to write a contract that specifies future employment and wages, perhaps as a function of the future environment. The market determines the relative bargaining positions of the agents but, other than that, plays little or no role in allocating labor services. The primary goals of the literature are to derive the properties shared by all efficient contracts and to investigate the employment implications of allocating labor in this manner. Finally, at least in the early studies, the terms of the contracts are treated as if they are binding.

(ii) Wage Rigidity

The framework of a typical contracting model can be described as follows. Each firm is tied to a number of workers, say N, for at least one period. This firm faces uncertainty about the economic environment in which it operates and must negotiate over working conditions with its employees before the uncertainty is resolved. The uncertainty is introduced by assuming that the firm's revenue (R), which depends on output and price, is given by the relationship $R(s) = sf(Lh)$ where $f(\ )$ represents an increasing, concave production function, s is a random variable, L denotes employment (so that $L \leq N$) and h represents hours worked.[4] The random variable s can be thought of as the price of the product or as a random element in labor productivity. In either case, s represents the state of nature with higher values corresponding to better economic conditions.

For now, we will assume that the distribution from which s is drawn is known by all parties at the time that the contract is drafted and that once the uncertainty is resolved, s is observable. In addition, we will assume that the terms of the contract are enforceable (these assumptions will be dropped later on). Since s is observable, it is possible to write contracts in which employment conditions are a function of s. For example, if the firm and its workers bargain over the hourly wage (w^e), employment (L), hours (h), and severance pay for laid-off workers (w^u), then the contract may specify different values for each of the variables for each possible realization of s.

To characterize the set of efficient contracts, consider the situation of a typical firm contemplating a contract consisting of the functions $\{w^e(s), w^u(s), L(s), h(s)\}$. If the firm accepts this contract and then state s occurs, it will employ $L(s)$ workers for $h(s)$ hours per day, pay its employed workers an hourly wage rate of $w^e(s)$ and pay its $[N - L(s)]$ laid-off workers $w^u(s)$ each. Its revenue will be $R(s) = sf(L(s)h(s))$, and therefore it will earn a profit of

$$(1) \qquad \pi(s) = sf(L(s)h(s)) - w^e(s)L(s)h(s) - w^u(s)[N - L(s)].$$

Expected profit, which is the value of the contract to the firm, is calculated by taking the expectation of (1) over s. Of course, the firm never accepts a contract that leads to negative expected profit.

Now consider the situation faced by the workers contemplating a contract offer by the firm. Each worker is assumed to have a utility function, $U(c,h)$, that is increasing in consumption and decreasing in hours worked (since an increase in hours worked necessitates a reduction in leisure). It is usually assumed that all income earned is spent on consumption. In other words, workers are not allowed to save. This assumption is not crucial to the analysis, but is made in order to capture the notion that savings are generally not adequate to smooth consumption optimally across economic states. Income and consumption expenditures are therefore equal to $w^e h$ when employed and w^u when laid off. Finally, if we assume that each worker is equally likely to be employed in any given state, then $p(s) = \dfrac{L(s)}{N}$ represents the probability that any given worker will be employed in state s. Expected utility if state s occurs is therefore given by

$$(2) \quad V(s) = p(s)U(w^e(s)h(s),h(s)) + [1 - p(s)]U(w^u(s),0).$$

The value of the contract to the worker is calculated by taking the expectation of (2) with respect to s. If we let $\underline{U}$ denote the level of expected utility that the worker could obtain by leaving the firm and seeking a job in the labor market, then the contract must provide at least this much utility to the worker, i.e., we must have $E_s V(s) \geq \underline{U}$ where E_s denotes the expectation over s.[5]

In general, a labor contract specifies values for w^e, L, h and w^u for each possible realization of s. However, in the initial implicit contract articles the firm was allowed to vary output only by hiring or firing workers. That is, hours worked were not allowed to vary. We refer to such contracts as "restricted" and begin by examining their features. This is accomplished by setting h equal to 1 if the worker is employed and 0 otherwise. The importance of restricting attention to such contracts is discussed in detail below. Finally, since the contract must be negotiated before the uncertainty is resolved, the form of the optimal contract will depend on attitudes towards risk. We begin by assuming that the worker is risk averse (U is concave) and that the firm is risk neutral (i.e., the firm is simply interested in maximizing expected profit).

An efficient restricted contract maximizes expected profit subject to a constraint on expected utility. We may state this formally using (1) and (2).

Definition: A restricted contract consists of three functions $w^e(s)$, $w^u(s)$, and $L(s)$ which describe wages, unemployment compensation, and employment as a function of s, the state of nature. The contract is *efficient* if it solves

   Max $E_s\pi(s)$ subject to $E_s V(s) \geq U^*$ and $E_s\pi(s) \geq 0$

for some $U^* \geq \underline{U}$, so that the workers achieve a level of expected utility at least as great as what they could obtain in the next best market alternative.

The major contribution of the early work by Bailey (1974) and Azariadis (1975) was the observation that in any efficient restricted contract, the hourly wage paid to employed workers is independent of the state of nature. In other words, the income earned by employed workers does not fluctuate with the economic conditions; wage rigidity is efficient. To understand the intuition behind this result, suppose that there are only two states of nature, s_1 and s_2, with $s_2 > s_1$ (the argument easily generalizes). Suppose further that the firm and its employees are considering a contract in which $w^e(s_1) \neq w^e(s_2)$. Then it can be shown that there exists another contract in which the wage paid to employed workers is constant across s_1 and s_2, which Pareto dominates this contract.

To construct this superior contract, let λ denote the probability that s_1 will occur. Then consider an alternative contract that is identical to the original except that instead of paying $w^e(s_1)$ if s_1 occurs and $w^e(s_2)$ if s_2 occurs, it pays

$$(3) \quad w^* = \frac{\lambda L(s_1)}{\lambda L(s_1) + (1-\lambda)L(s_2)} w^e(s_1) + \frac{(1-\lambda)L(s_2)}{\lambda L(s_1) + (1-\lambda)L(s_2)} w^e(s_2)$$

in both states. This wage is constructed so that the firm's expected wage bill is the same in both contracts. In the initial, variable wage contract, the firm hires $L(s_1)$ workers and pays a wage of $w^e(s_1)$ with probability λ. With probability $(1-\lambda)$ the firm hires $L(s_2)$ workers and pays $w^e(s_2)$. This leads to an expected wage bill of $\lambda L(s_1)w^e(s_1) + (1-\lambda) L(s_2)w^e(s_2)$. In the alternative, fixed-wage contract, the firm's hiring practices are the same, however, it pays w^* in each state. Thus, its expected wage bill is $[\lambda L(s_1) + (1 - \lambda)L(s_2)]w^*$. Simple algebra reveals (using (3)) that the two wage bills are identical.

We are now in position to compare the relative welfare of the parties under the two contracts. Since employment, unemployment compensation and the expected wage bill are the same for both contracts, the firm's expected profit would not change if the second contract were substituted for the first. Therefore, the firm is indifferent between the variable and fixed-wage contracts.

This is not the case for the workers. A typical worker is employed in state i with probability $p(s_i) = L(s_i)/N$. Expected utility under the variable-wage contract (EU_v) is therefore

(4) $EU_v = \lambda\{p(s_1)U(w^e(s_1),1) + [1 - p(s_1)]U(w^u(s_1),0)\} +$
$(1 - \lambda)\{p(s_2)U(w^e(s_2),1) + [1 - p(s_2)]U(w^u(s_2),0)\}.$

Under the fixed-wage contract, expected utility is equal to (4) with w^* replacing $w^e(s_1)$ and $w^e(s_2)$. If we let EU_f denote this value and make the appropriate substitution, we obtain

$EU_f = [\lambda p(s_1) + (1 - \lambda)p(s_2)]U(w^*,1) + \lambda[1 - p(s_1)]U(w^u(s_1),0) +$
$(1 - \lambda)[1 - p(s_2)]U(w^u(s_2),0).$

In order to compare these two values we begin by noting that severance pay and the employment probabilities do not differ across the contracts. Therefore, $EU_f > EU_v$ if

$[\lambda p(s_1) + (1 - \lambda)p(s_2)]U(w^*,1) > \lambda p(s_1)U(w^e(s_1),1) +$
$(1 - \lambda)p(s_2)U(w^e(s_2),1).$

If we define $z = \dfrac{\lambda p(s_1)}{\lambda p(s_1) + (1 - \lambda)p(s_2)}$ then this equation is

equivalent to

$U(w^*,1) > zU(w^e(s_1),1) + (1 - z)U(w^e(s_2),1).$

Finally, if we substitute the value of w^* into the left-hand side we obtain

$$U(zw^e(s_1) + (1 - z)w^e(s_2),1) > zU(w^e(s_1),1) + (1 - z)U(w^e(s_2),1)$$

which holds due to the concavity of the utility function. Therefore, due to the risk aversion of the workers, $EU_f > EU_v$. That is, the workers benefit from switching to the fixed-wage contract.

The reason for this is rather simple and is illustrated in figure 4.1. The variable-wage contract represents a gamble to the workers since the hourly wage varies with the random variable s. As is well known, any risk-averse agent would prefer to receive the expected value of a gamble with certainty rather than face the gamble itself. But this is exactly what the fixed-wage contract offers. Thus, the employees prefer the contract with a rigid wage and, since the firm earns the same expected profit under the two contracts, the fixed-wage contract Pareto dominates the variable-wage contract.

Figure 4.1

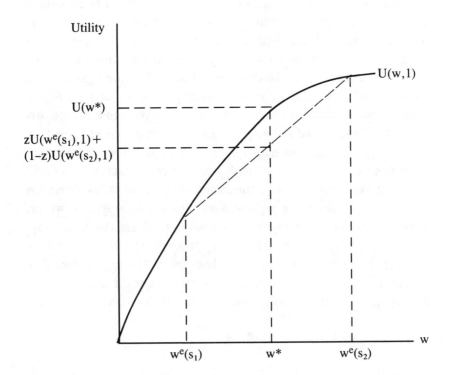

In this model, the primary role of the wage rate is to allocate risk optimally across the firm and its workers; it does not adjust to clear the labor market. Since firms are risk neutral, they are willing to provide insurance to their risk-averse workers by offering a wage rate that is independent of economic conditions. The firm benefits by doing so since by offering a fixed-wage contract it can lower its expected wage bill while at the same time providing its workers with the same level of expected utility that they would receive in a comparable variable-wage contract.

Can this model explain layoff unemployment? This is equivalent to asking whether efficient restricted contracts are ever characterized by $L(s) < N$ for any s. That is, does the firm lay off workers during some states of nature? At first blush it would seem like we should be able to construct an argument similar to the one we used above (to prove that wage rigidity is efficient) to show that the firm would always fully employ its workforce. After all, if workers want to avoid risk with respect to the hourly wage, why would they be willing to accept risk with respect to employment? In spite of the intuitive appeal of this argument, there are cases in which it is incorrect. The reason is that, if hours cannot be varied, the firm is less willing to provide full insurance in employment than wages. When compensation is at issue, the firm can be persuaded to pay a wage above labor's marginal revenue product during bad states by allowing it to pay less than labor's value during good states. No such trade-off exists with respect to employment. Suppose, for example, that the contract on the table includes layoffs in a particularly bad state of nature and full employment in all other states. If the firm were to agree to increase employment in the layoff state, it could not be compensated by lowering employment in other states without producing unemployment in those alternative states. Instead, the firm must be compensated by allowing it to lower the hourly wage. However, workers may not be willing to trade a pay cut for less risk in employment. Whether or not the trade actually takes place will depend on the workers' level of risk aversion and how much of a pay cut the firm demands in order to fully employ labor in all states. It can be shown that layoffs are efficient only if the workers are not too risk averse and if the firm has a strong desire to reduce its workforce during adverse conditions (see, for example, Azariadis 1975 or Cooper 1987). Unfortunately (at least as far as this theory of unemployment is concerned), even when layoffs *are* efficient, the act of distributing risk optimally across firms and workers results in fewer layoffs than would occur in pure market economy; allocating labor via contracts leads to *overemployment.*[6]

In summary, the major contribution of the early articles on labor contracts was to draw attention to the fact that wage rigidity could be expected to arise as an equilibrium phenomenon in some situations. Unfortunately, in the framework chosen, wage rigidity is not always compatible with layoff unemployment and, even when the two are compatible, contracts actually reduce the number of layoffs one would expect to observe.

(iii) Other Difficulties

There are two other troubling aspects of the basic model. First, it is not clear that the agents can be trusted to abide by the implicit agreement once the uncertainty has been resolved. An efficient contract requires that workers sacrifice income in good states in order to keep their income from falling during poor states. The reduction in pay during good states is equivalent to an insurance premium that must be paid in order to guarantee that the firm will pay the worker more than the marginal revenue product of labor when poor economic conditions arise. However, suppose that a good state occurs. What incentive does the worker have to carry out his or her part of the implicit agreement? Why not quit and seek employment at a wage commensurate with his or her true market value? If such a job is available on the spot market, then there is no reason for the worker to continue the relationship with the firm. One way around this problem is to add an additional constraint to the contracting problem that requires the firm to pay the worker no less than what could be earned by quitting and seeking a job on the spot market in each state of nature. We will discuss how this alters the nature of the contract in the next section.

The second problem concerns the *ad hoc* restriction on hours worked. It is not at all clear why the firm and its employees would not wish
to bargain over hours. This is especially true if by doing so they could
achieve a settlement that dominates the optimal restricted contract. On
the other hand, if it can be shown that efficient restricted and unrestricted
contracts share many important features, e.g., wage rigidity and the
possibility of layoff unemployment, then this simplifying assumption
may not be so troublesome. Unfortunately, this is not the case. Efficient unrestricted contracts *never* include layoffs and may not be consistent with wage rigidity.

To see how allowing hours to be an object of negotiation affects the
contracting process, we begin by defining precisely what we mean by
an "efficient unrestricted contract."

Definition: An *efficient unrestricted contract* consists of four functions
$w^e(s)$, $w^u(s)$, $L(s)$ and $h(s)$ which describe the hourly wage, severance
pay, employment and hours as a function of s, the state of nature. In
addition, these functions solve

Max $E_s\pi(s)$ subject to $E_sV(s) \geq U^*$ and $E_s\pi(s) \geq 0$
for some $U^* \geq \underline{U}$.

Solving this maximization problem requires the use of optimal control theory, and therefore, we will not describe the actual procedure
used to characterize these contracts. Instead, we will list some of the
more interesting properties and discuss the implications for wages and
employment.

First, in any efficient unrestricted contract, employed labor's marginal
utility of consumption must be equal across all states. With risk-averse
workers, this can only be accomplished by providing these workers with
the same level of compensation (and hence consumption) under all
economic conditions.[7] It is also worth noting that, as in the case of
restricted contracts, this is equivalent to the firm providing complete
insurance along one dimension—consumption. However, complete insurance in consumption need not imply wage rigidity when hours can
vary. To see this, simply note that compensation in state s to employed

workers is equal to $w^e(s)h(s)$. If hours cannot vary, the only way to keep this value constant across states is to make $w^e(s)$ independent of s (thereby generating wage rigidity). If h can vary, the firm can render consumption state independent by paying higher wages in periods in which it wants labor to work fewer hours. Consequently, contract theory cannot explain wage rigidity without applying the restrictive assumption that hours worked are not negotiable.

Turn next to employment. It can be shown that efficient unrestricted contracts never involve layoffs (see, for example, Cooper 1987). In other words, the firm always fully utilizes its labor force so that workers are completely insured against risk in the other major dimension—employment status. The reason for this is actually rather straightforward. Since workers are risk averse, they would (*ex ante*) be willing to reduce their hours worked during poor states in return for guaranteed employment. Increasing employment and reducing hours in a manner that keeps total labor services constant assures that the firm will be willing to allow the work-sharing arrangement. Therefore, by agreeing to allow hours worked to vary directly with economic conditions, labor can avoid the risk of being laid off. In addition, once hours are fixed, wages can then be adjusted to keep income and consumption constant as well. In essence, by setting up work-sharing arrangements, management can provide labor with almost complete insurance (leisure still varies with s).

Another way to view this second result is as follows. We argued above that workers will want to avoid employment risk for the same reason that they want to avoid risk in consumption. However, if hours cannot vary, the firm is not always willing to provide insurance along this dimension. Allowing hours worked to vary provides the firm with increased flexibility in the negotiating process and results in a superior contract. In periods in which labor's value to the firm is low, full employment can be maintained while at the same time allowing the firm to cut back on its wage bill by reducing hours.

These two results represent a major setback for those who had hoped that the theory of implicit contracts would provide an explanation of wage rigidity and unemployment. In the most general setting (with hours flexible), optimal risk-sharing is not consistent with layoff unemployment and may not lead to wage rigidity. This problem can be avoided by noting that in most contract talks, hours worked are not considered negotiable. Therefore, it may seem reasonable to simply assume that hours cannot vary. This, however, is not a satisfactory solution. After all, even if we do not observe contracts that provide for flexible hours, a theory of optimal contracts should be able to explain why, in spite of the fact that unrestricted contracts are superior to restricted contracts, such agreements do not emerge from the negotiating process.

Finally, it is worth emphasizing once again that even when hours are fixed exogenously, efficient risk-sharing may still be incompatible with layoff unemployment. If workers are sufficiently risk averse, then the optimal contract is characterized by full employment regardless of economic conditions. In addition, even in the cases in which layoffs are optimal, risk-sharing through long-term contracts actually reduces the number of layoffs we would expect to observe. We can conclude that to use contract theory to explain both wage rigidity and unemployment, the basic model would have to be altered in some nontrivial manner.

B. Extensions of the Basic Model

(i) Asymmetric Information

One of the more unrealistic assumptions of the basic model is the supposition that the uncertain parameter s (the state of nature) is observable by both parties. In reality, since s determines the value of labor to the firm, it is likely to be the case that the firm is better informed about the true value of s than its employees. This observation has led a number of authors to consider the implications of informational asymmetries for the contracting procedure (see, for example, Hall and Lilien 1979 and the papers in the supplement of the *Quarterly Journal of Economics* 1983). When informational asymmetries are present, it becomes difficult to implement contracts in which wages, hours, and employment are state-contingent since the uninformed party (usually labor) may have good reason not to trust the informed party (usually management) to truthfully reveal the state of nature. For example, suppose that in the optimal contract hours are increasing in s and compensation is independent of s. Then, if labor cannot observe s, the firm would have an incentive to announce that the best state has occurred regardless of the truth (this leads to the largest value for h and the lowest value for w, thereby yielding the largest profit for the firm). To keep the firm from misrepresenting the true state, the contract must be structured so that it is always in the interest of the firm to tell the truth. Constraints added to the contracting problem to induce truth telling are referred to as "incentive compatibility constraints." As we will see below, by extending the basic model in this manner, underemployment may arise as a feature of an efficient contract.

To make this precise, consider a simplified version of the basic model in which the firm bargains with a single worker over compensation (c) and hours (h). In this case, profit for the firm in state $\overset{\times}{s}$ if it announces that state s has occurred is given by $\pi(s|\hat{s}) = \hat{s}f(h(s)) - c(s)$. Then the firm will always tell the truth if $\pi(\overset{\times}{s}|\overset{\times}{s}) \geq \pi(s|\hat{s})$ for all $\hat{s}$. This equation states that the firm always earns more profit from telling the truth than from misrepresenting the true state. If this condition is met, then contracts can be written and enforced in which the terms of the contract are state-dependent. This is formalized in the following definition.

Definition: An *efficient incentive compatible contract* consists of a compensation schedule $c(s)$ and a schedule of hours $h(s)$ that solve

Max $E_s\pi(s)$ subject to $E_sU[c(s),h(s)] \geq U^*$, $E_s\pi(s) \geq 0$
and $\pi(\overset{\times}{s}|\overset{\times}{s}) \geq \pi(s|\overset{\times}{s})$ for all $\hat{s}$

for some $U^* \geq \underline{U}$.

The major insights provided by this line of work can be illustrated in a model with two possible states of nature, s_1 and s_2 with $s_1 < s_2$. For the worker, utility is increasing in c and decreasing in h. Assuming that the utility function is quasiconcave, the indifference curves take the form depicted in figure 4.2a. Holding h fixed, utility increases with

c so that higher indifference curves are associated with greater levels of utility.

Iso-profit curves for the firm are depicted in figure 4.2b. Combinations of c and h yielding the same level of profit satisfy $sf(h) - c = z$ where z is an arbitrary constant. Since $f(h)$ is concave, the iso-profit curves increase at a decreasing rate with a slope that is increasing in s (solving the equation above for c gives us the iso-profit equation: $c = sf(h) - z$ so that the slope of the curve is $sf'(h)$). Each value of s generates a whole family of iso-profit curves with steeper curves representing better economic conditions (in figure 4.2b, the dashed curves denote the iso-profit curves in the good state and the solid lines represent the curves in the bad state). With h fixed, profit is decreasing in c so that lower iso-profit curves are associated with greater profit for the firm.

If s could be observed by both the firm and its employees, an efficient contract would result in a tangency between the iso-profit and indifference curves in each state of nature. Three examples of what an efficient unrestricted contract might look like are provided in figures 4.3a–4.3c. In each case $x(s_1)$ denotes the terms of the contract if state s_1 occurs. Consider figure 4.3a first. In this case, compensation and hours worked are both higher in the good state. Moreover, if the bad state (s_1) occurs (implying that the correct iso-profit curves are the flatter set), then the firm is better off at point $x(s_1)$ than it would be at point $x(s_2)$. To see this, note that the flat iso-profit curve intersecting $x(s_2)$ is higher and therefore represents lower profit than the flat curve intersecting $x(s_1)$. By a similar argument, if the good state occurs (implying that the true iso-profit curves are the steeper set), then the firm would rather be at $x(s_2)$ than at $x(s_1)$.

Why is this important? Suppose now that s is observable only by the firm. Then this efficient contract can be implemented only if the worker can trust the firm to reveal the truth once the uncertainty has been resolved. In figure 4.3a the firm never has an incentive to lie and thus there is no reason for the worker to distrust the firm. This is so because regardless of the economic conditions, the firm earns a larger profit from telling the truth than it would from lying. In this case the incen-

Figure 4.2a

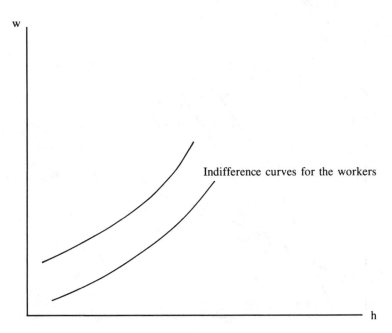

Figure 4.2b

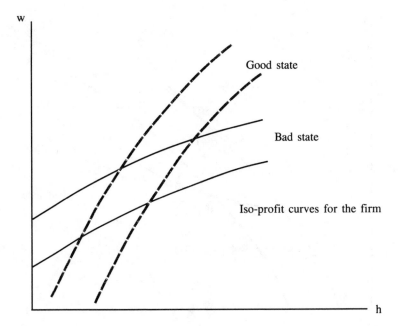

Figure 4.3a

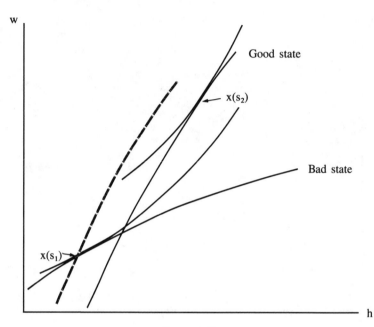

Figure 4.3b

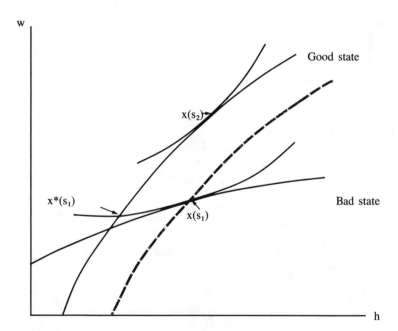

tive compatibility constraints are satisfied by the efficient contract and the existence of asymmetric information does not affect the outcome of the negotiations.

This is not the case in figure 4.3b. Here the firm has an incentive to lie if the good state occurs. To see this, note that in the good state $x(s_1)$ lies on a better iso-profit curve than $x(s_2)$. Consequently, if the firm can convince its workers that s_1 has occurred when in fact s_2 has occurred, it can operate at $x(s_1)$ rather than at $x(s_2)$ and earn greater profit (as drawn, at $x(s_1)$ the firm gets its employees to work approximately the same number of hours as at $x(s_2)$ but at less pay). This means that it is in the firm's interest to claim that state s_1 has occurred regardless of the true economic conditions. Since the efficient unrestricted contract does not satisfy the incentive compatibility constraints (in particular $\pi(s_1|s_2) \geq \pi(s_2|s_2)$), it cannot be enforced when s is known only by the firm. A similar situation exists in figure 4.3c where the firm has an incentive to lie in the bad state, i.e., $\pi(s_2|s_1) \geq \pi(s_1|s_1)$ so that the firm makes more profit in state s_1 if it claims that s_2 has occurred.

Figure 4.3c

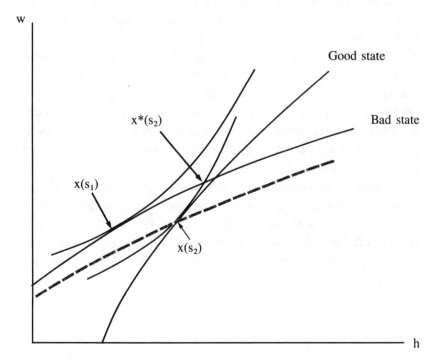

When asymmetric information is present and the optimal unrestricted contract does not satisfy the incentive compatibility constraints, the contract must be altered in order to remove the firm's incentive to misrepresent the state of nature. In figure 4.3b, the firm always wants to announce that the poor state has occurred so that it can compensate the worker less for approximately the same number of hours worked. One way to remove the incentive to lie when s_2 occurs is to restrict the hours worked in state s_1. For example, the firm and worker could agree to replace $x(s_1)$ with the (c,h) package represented by $x^*(s_1)$. Since $x^*(s_1)$ lies on the same steep iso-profit curve as $x(s_2)$, the firm will then be willing to tell the truth when the good state occurs. Note that in order to satisfy the incentive compatibility constraints, hours worked must be reduced.[8] Thus, in this case asymmetric information results in less hours worked or *underemployment*. It is important to note that this is not an explanation of unemployment, since the workers are never laid off completely. Instead, work hours are reduced in poor states below the values that would emerge in a contract without informational problems.

Since the optimal unrestricted contract leads the firm to lie when the bad state occurs in figure 4.3c, the terms of the contract in the good state must be altered in order to satisfy the incentive compatibility constraints. This can be accomplished by replacing $x(s_2)$ with $x^*(s_2)$, thereby requiring employees to work additional hours in the good state. Since labor is more valuable in the good state, the firm can afford to compensate the workers for the extra hours if s_2 occurs but not if state s_1 occurs. Consequently, the firm will accurately reveal the value of s once the uncertainty has been resolved. In this case, asymmetric information results in a contract calling for more hours worked. We refer to this as *overemployment*.

Figure 4.3c also differs from 4.3a and 4.3b in one other manner. In the first two examples the worker prefers for the good state to occur since $x(s_2)$ lies on a higher indifference curve than $x(s_1)$. Unfortunately, in figure 4.3c the worker is better off in the bad state. This perverse result must leave one with an uncomfortable feeling about the overemployment case.

Figure 4.3 indicates that asymmetric information may have no impact on the optimal contract or it may result in overemployment or underemployment. If it results in underemployment, then contract theory combined with informational problems can explain why economies may get struck in less than full employment equilibria. Unfortunately, the following theorem from Green and Kahn (1983) indicates that underemployment is an unlikely result.

Theorem: The optimal unrestricted contract satisfies the incentive compatibility constraints if the demand for leisure is independent of income. If leisure is a normal good, then the optimal incentive compatible contract results in overemployment. If leisure is inferior, then the optimal incentive compatible contract is characterized by underemployment.

Since empirical studies consistently report that leisure is a normal good, this theorem is rather disappointing. It indicates that private information held by the firm is likely to result in greater utilization of labor—not less. Therefore, we cannot rely on this model (as is) for an explanation of unemployment or underemployment. In addition, as we saw above, when overemployment occurs workers actually prefer poor economic conditions over good ones. This runs counter to observation and severely weakens the value of the model.

There have been several recent attempts to modify the asymmetric model in order to circumvent these problems. Grossman and Hart (1981) accomplish this by ruling out work-sharing and by changing the assumptions concerning attitudes towards risk; they assume that workers are risk neutral and firms are risk averse. In this setting, workers bear the risk and the optimal restricted contract tends to equalize expected profit across states of nature rather than wages. However, to equalize profit, wages must be higher in good states than in bad ones and, therefore, since hours are fixed, the firm has a strong incentive to lie whenever good states occur (so that it may pay a lower wage). The only way to remove this incentive is to make wages state-independent as well. But, the firm will only be willing to stabilize the wage if it can reduce employment in poor states. Thus, the optimal restricted incentive-compatible contract results in layoffs in bad states. Unfortunately, this result depends on the rather unusual assumption concerning the relative attitudes towards risk of the workers and the firm. It also relies on the *ad hoc* assumption that work-sharing arrangements cannot be instituted.

An alternative, more appealing approach to dealing with these problems has recently been offered by Cooper (1985) and Moore (1985). They demonstrate that when workers are better informed about the true state of nature than are firms, efficient incentive-compatible contracts may, under reasonable conditions, be characterized by underemployment. The basic idea is as follows. Suppose that s is nonstochastic but that the employees' disutility from work varies with economic conditions and is known only by the workers. This makes utility a random variable as far as the firm is concerned. In order to get the workers to accurately reveal their tastes once the uncertainty has been resolved, incentive compatibility constraints must be added to the basic contracting framework. If we assume that work-sharing is not feasible, then, as in the Grossman-Hart model above, the incentive compatibility constraints imply that the wage must be independent of the state of nature (otherwise the worker would announce that the state with the highest wage has occurred regardless of the truth). But, if the wage is fixed and the disutility from work varies with economic conditions, employment states are risky for workers. Efficiency therefore results in less employment than we would observe if tastes were publicly observed.

Models in which workers possess superior information about the economic environment are still in their early stages of development. The initial studies, e.g., Cooper (1985) and Moore (1985), indicate that the structure of preferences and the manner in which uncertainty affects worker preferences play important roles in determining the nature of the optimal contract. For example, restrictions must be placed on how worker indifference curves shift as economic conditions change in order to solve even the simplest contracting problem. Therefore, although the early results seem promising, we will have to wait and see how productive this line of research will be in the future. For a more detailed discussion of the issues involved, readers are referred to Cooper (1987).

(ii) Implementation Problems

As we noted above, although the literature has focused on implicit contracts (contracts which are not binding), most papers simply assume that the two parties involved will honor the contract once the uncertainty has been resolved. However, since efficiency usually dictates that the worker be paid less than the marginal revenue product in some states, i.e., the worker pays an insurance premium, and more than the marginal revenue product in other states, i.e., the worker collects insurance, each party faces an incentive to break the contract in at least one instance. Therefore, unless we assume that these contracts can be enforced through legal action, the basic model must be extended in some manner to make sure that the contract can be implemented.

One method for accomplishing this is to add reputation considerations to the model. For example, a worker who quits often will earn a reputation as a quitter and will have difficulty finding a job. Or a firm that fails to honor its part of the implicit agreement will find it difficult to find workers willing to accept employment. In both cases, the party choosing to sever the relationship runs the risk of developing a reputation as "untrustworthy." These reputation effects can be strong enough to ensure that the contract will be honored (see Carmichael (1984) or Bull (1987) for an example of this type of argument).

An alternative way to solve the enforcement problem is to build incentives into the contract that will ensure that it will be in the interest of both parties to honor the terms under all conditions. Suppose, for example, that when the worker is hired, a contract is negotiated which sets the wage to be paid during training (w_t) and a wage to be paid once training is completed ($w^e(s)$). The post-training wage is a function of the unknown parameter s, the state of nature. Suppose further that during the training period the worker acquires firm-specific human capital and that work-sharing is not feasible. In such a setting and in the absence of enforcement problems, any efficient contract would specify the same w^e for all s. Now, let $w^m(s)$ denote the market wage (what the worker could earn by quitting and seeking employment on the spot market) so that if the firm wants to retain the worker's services, it must offer a contract satisfying $w^e(s) \geq w^m(s)$ for all s. Not surprisingly, it can be shown that for sufficiently high s, the optimal unrestricted contract dictates a wage below $w^m(s)$. To satisfy the added constraint, the firm must pay the market wage in a good state and find some other way to collect the insurance premium. This can be accomplished by lowering the training wage, thereby collecting part of the premium before the uncertainty is resolved. This produces a contract with a wage that is flexible upwards (since $w^e(s)$ is increasing in s if s is sufficiently high) but rigid downward. Interested readers are referred to Holmstrom (1983) or Ioannides and Pissarides (1983) for more details.

C. What Next?

Contract theory began as an attempt to provide a microeconomic foundation for wage rigidity. In this regard, it has succeeded (at least to some extent) in that it has demonstrated that when wages are isolated from market forces and used as an instrument to allocate risk across a risk-neutral firm and its risk-averse workers, wage rigidity is an efficient outcome. By stabilizing the wage, workers are able to insure themselves against perverse economic conditions. The firm is willing to provide this insurance since by doing so it can reduce its wage bill below what it would have to pay in a variable-wage contract. Unfortunately, the same type of arguments that lead to this conclusion imply that efficient contracts should also reduce the riskiness faced by workers in other dimensions; in particular, in employment status. Therefore, contract theory has been unable to explain the coexistence of wage rigidity and layoff unemployment.

As we have seen above, the basic model can be altered in a number of ways to generate some of the desired results. For example, by adding asymmetric information, the possibility of an underemployment equilibrium emerges. In most cases, however, the extensions seem forced. Some times the new models are able to explain one phenomenon (layoff unemployment) but lose the ability to explain others (wage rigidity). In other instances, the new models succeed only by making assumptions directly opposed to empirical findings. And finally, in some cases, success is achieved at a much lower level than originally desired (asymmetric information models provide an explanation for *underemployment* not *unemployment*).

This is not to say that this literature is not valuable. There can be no doubt that recent empirical findings do suggest that there are strong attachments between firms and their workers that are likely to render wage rates somewhat immune to market forces. Consequently, it is important for us to understand how wages and employment will be determined in these long-term relationships. What we *can* conclude from all of this is that contract theory *on its own* will probably never produce a satisfactory theory of unemployment. By embedding the basic contracting model in a framework consistent with equilibrium unemployment, we may be able to obtain some valuable insights into matters such as the role of risk-sharing in cyclical variations in unemployment. Examples of recent attempts to do just this are Hosios (1986) and Arnott, Hosios, and Stiglitz (1988).

D. Policy Implications

In spite of its failure to provide an explanation for both wage rigidity and unemployment, there have been a number of attempts to draw policy conclusions from contracting models. Two distinct approaches have been employed. First, there have been studies in which it is assumed that labor is allocated using simple fixed-length, fixed nominal wage contracts with employment set *ex post* by the firm (see, for example, Gray 1976, Fisher 1977, Taylor 1980, and Gertler 1982). These models have been used to study the effectiveness of monetary policy, the optimality of certain monetary policy regimes and the time-series properties of employment, output and prices in a contracting framework. One important result was to show that in the presence of long-term contracts, i.e., more than one period, anticipated changes in the money supply could have real effects. This result remains true even when the wage level is indexed to the price level. These models differ from those reviewed above in that the assumed structure of the contract is not optimal. Due to this lack of microfoundations, Cooper (1987) refers to this line of research as "macro-contracting models."

The second approach builds upon the micro-contracting models of sections A–C to investigate the policy implications of efficient contracts. To begin, consider the question of whether or not money is neutral. Azariadis (1978) and Cooper (1988) have both investigated this issue by analyzing models in which the economy is subject to both permanent and temporary and real and nominal shocks. Agents attempt to use prices to infer the types of shocks that have occurred, but price signals are incomplete (note that a crucial assumption is that the underlying shocks are not observable). The contracts allowed are fairly flexible. For example, although wages are negotiated in nominal terms, they can be indexed to prices, if desired. Nevertheless, as long as price signals are incomplete, money is not neutral. Changes in the money supply cause prices to change, but since these price changes may be the result of temporary shocks, it is not optimal to fully index wages to prices.

Turning to labor market policies, there have been several studies of the impact of unemployment insurance programs in a contracting framework. Polemarchakis and Weiss (1978) consider a simple two-sector general equilibrium contracting model in which it is costly for workers to switch sectors. Since, in general, optimal contracts result in compensation that differs from marginal productivity, labor will not be allocated efficiently across sectors. They demonstrate that when random shifts in demand dictate that workers should switch sectors, the market will result in too little mobility. This is essentially due to monopoly power—an increase in demand leads a firm to want to increase its labor force; but, since this would require increasing the wage it pays its current employees as well, the firm does not expand as much as is optimal. The government can reduce the inefficiency by subsidizing job movements. One effective way to do so is to have the government fund part of the unemployment insurance program.

Kahn (1985) takes a different tack. He considers a model in which the worker's outside wage is random and cannot be observed by the firm. In addition, the firm is subject to random productivity shocks. As one would expect, an optimal contract results in a larger differential between the wage and severance pay when labor productivity is high. The reason is simple: the worker is more valuable to the firm when productivity is high. Therefore, to keep the worker from quitting, the firm must increase the spread between the wage and unemployment insurance.

The final policy issue concerns the uniqueness of equilibrium. As we have already seen in the two previous chapters, search and market power can lead to a situation in which multiple, Pareto-rankable equilibria may exist. This opens up the possibility that the economy may get stuck in a low-employment equilibrium. Government action might then be required to push the economy towards full employment. Not surprisingly, this possibility emerges in the contracts literature as well. Hosios (1986) demonstrates this possibility by considering a contract model in which laid-off workers can search for employment and might be hired *ex post* by firms. He demonstrates that multiple Pareto-rankable equilibria may exist. As in the search literature, this is due to an externality and a feedback mechanism. When a firm lays off a worker, it reduces the cost of other firms hiring labor in the *ex post* market (by increasing the supply of labor in the *ex post* market). However, this also increases the amount of activity in the *ex post* market—a factor that bolsters the outside opportunities of labor. This leads to greater market power for workers in the negotiation process, and therefore makes layoffs more profitable. The policy implications are then similar to those outlined at the end of chapter 2.

NOTES

1. See, for example, the discussion in Stiglitz (1986).

2. There are several excellent, more detailed surveys of the implicit contracts literature available including Azariadis (1981), Hart (1983), Rosen (1985), Stiglitz (1986), and Cooper (1987). Much of this chapter is based on the discussions in Stiglitz (1986) and Cooper (1987).

3. We do not have to assume that bargaining actually takes place. Instead we could assume that firms offer contracts that workers accept or reject. Profit-maximizing firms will always offer efficient contracts.

4. Labor is assumed to be the only productive input. Note also that since $f(\ )$ depends on total labor hours, we are assuming that labor services (in terms of employment) and hours worked are perfect substitutes. These assumptions are not crucial to the analysis.

5. Almost all of the initial articles take $\underline{U}$ as given and focus on the interaction between a specific firm and its employees. Since the remainder of the labor market is ignored, these papers do not provide an equilibrium analysis. Azariadis (1975) demonstrated that the model could be closed

by varying $\underline{U}$ and solving the optimal contract problem to trace out supply and demand for labor schedules. The intersection of supply and demand determines the market-clearing $\underline{U}$ and the distribution of workers across firms. The wages that correspond to $\underline{U}$ can then be considered, in a sense, market-clearing wages. For an alternative, search-theoretic approach to closing the model, see Hosios (1986).

6. In a market economy with labor traded on a spot market, each firm hires workers such that the marginal revenue product of the last worker hired equals the wage. Let w^s denote the spot market wage. Then L^s, spot market employment, satisfies $sf'(L^s) = w^s$. Layoffs occur as s falls but the wage always adjusts to produce full employment. For a proof that $L^s \leq L(s)$ see, for example, Cooper (1987).

7. This statement is true *provided* that utility is separable in compensation and hours. If the utility function is not separable, then compensation (and hence wages) will not be constant across states.

8. In figure 4.3b it may appear that the incentive to lie could also be removed by replacing $x(s_1)$ with the (c,h) package at the intersection of the good state iso-profit curve and the indifference curve that intersects $x(s_1)$. This would represent an increase in compensation and hours worked in the bad state. However, the firm earns greater profit at $x^*(s_1)$ than at this alternative point and since both points lie on the same worker indifference curve, $x^*(s_1)$ Pareto dominates this alternative.

5
More on Wage Rigidity
Efficiency Wages and Insider/Outsider Workers

A. Introduction

Due to the failure of contract theory to provide a consistent explanation of wage rigidity *and* unemployment, a number of new theories have recently been developed to fill this important gap in the literature. Most of these theories adopt the same microeconomic approach taken in the contract literature in that they seek to explain wage rigidity and unemployment as a natural outcome in a setting in which rational, utility, and profit-maximizing agents operate. While it is far too early to assess the overall success of this work, the initial insights that have been provided seem promising.

In this chapter I briefly outline the basic tenets of (what I consider to be) the two most promising lines of research in this area: efficiency wage theory and the insider/outsider theory of unemployment. In each case, I will focus on the assumptions used to explain wage rigidity and the link between wage rigidity and unemployment. I will also attempt to point out the weaknesses and any logical inconsistencies that remain. This will provide some guidance as to the directions these literatures are likely to take in the future. Since both literatures are in their early stages of development, the treatments offered in this chapter will be somewhat more succinct than those offered in the previous chapters. This is not meant to indicate that this work is less important, merely that the profession has had less time to develop these ideas fully. A brief discussion of some of the policy implications that can be gleaned from the early models concludes the chapter.

B. Efficiency Wages

The fundamental assumption of efficiency wage theory is that the labor productivity is positively related to the wage rate. A number of possible reasons have been suggested to support this claim, the most prominent of which are discussed in detail below. Regardless of the reason, once this claim is accepted, it is not difficult to produce a model with wage rigidity and unemployment. The argument is as follows. Suppose that at the current wage rate there is an excess supply of labor. Then, although there are workers available who are willing to work for less than the going wage, firms may not want to cut the wage rate since by doing so they would trigger a reduction in productivity and (possibly) lower profit. It is therefore possible for equilibrium to be characterized by an excess supply of labor even though the wage rate is positive.

This argument can be illustrated using a simple model from Solow (1979, 1980).[1] Let n denote employment; e, worker efficiency (a measure of productivity); w, the nominal wage; and p, the price level. Then the basic tenet of efficiency wage theory is that e depends on the real wage. Profit for the firm is given by

(1) $\pi = pF(e(\frac{w}{p})n) - wn$

where $F(\ )$ denotes the production function. That is, total output depends on total efficiency units supplied by labor. In this setting, the firm's optimization problem is to choose n and w to maximize profits. Differentiating π with respect to n yields the familiar condition that determines the demand for labor: the firm hires labor until the real wage ($\frac{w}{p}$) equals the marginal product of the last worker hired (eF'). Differentiating with respect to w yields what has been referred to as the "Solow condition"

(2) $\frac{e'}{e} \frac{w}{p} = 1.$

This equation defines the optimal wage. It states that the firm should set the wage rate such that the elasticity of the efficiency function with respect to the wage is equal to 1. The solution to (2) is known as the "efficiency wage" since it is the wage rate that minimizes labor costs per efficiency unit of labor. For simplicity, assume that all firms are identical so that they all offer the same efficiency wage, w^*.[2] Then, if at w^* the supply of labor exceeds demand, the wage will not fall and unemployment will emerge. This follows even though there are workers available who are willing to work for a wage below w^*. Firms are unwilling to hire these workers because they realize that lowering the wage will result in a more than proportional reduction in e, which will lower profit. The basic problem is that the workers who could be hired for less would not be as productive as those currently employed (not due to inherent difference in the workers but simply because they would not work as hard) and therefore replacing the current labor force with cheaper labor would not be profitable.

This simple model highlights the importance of the hypothesis that productivity is tied to the wage rate. Without this assumption, firms would attempt to pay the lowest wage that workers would accept and equilibrium would occur only when the wage had been driven down to its market-clearing level; there would be no unemployment. It is therefore crucial for the proponents of efficiency wage theory to provide a reasonable justification for this assumed functional relationship.

The idea that such a link exists and has important implications for unemployment actually has ancient roots. For example, Bowles (1985) traces the notion as far back as Marx's theory of the reserved army of the unemployed. However, most of the literature cites Leibenstein (1957), who was interested in explaining wage rigidity and unemployment in underdeveloped countries, as the first individual to suggest that such a link exists. Leibenstein argued that workers earning higher wages would be able to achieve a higher level of nutrition and would therefore be ill less often. While this argument seems reasonable for underdeveloped areas, it is probably not a very important factor in developed countries. Nevertheless, several other reasons have been suggested that would account for this link in modern economies. In the remainder of this chapter, I focus on one particular explanation due to Shapiro and Stiglitz (1984)—that better paid workers work harder to avoid being fired.[3] I have chosen this model for a number of reasons, including its simplicity, intuitive appeal, and popularity in the profession. A number of other theories (some quite similar in structure to the Shapiro/Stiglitz approach) are discussed in Akerlof and Yellin (1986, pp. 4-9) and Katz (1986a, pp. 240-251).

(i) Endogenous Effort and Unemployment

Suppose that at each instant the wage rate adjusts to clear the labor market so that every willing worker is guaranteed employment. Why would a worker expend any effort on the job? After all, effort generates disutility and even if the worker is fired for lack of work, a new job could be obtained at the same (market-clearing) wage without delay. Such behavior, loafing on the job, has been commonly referred to in this literature as "shirking." Without unemployment, there would be no cost to shirking, and firms would be unable to induce their employees to put out any effort at all. Therefore, zero unemployment is not consistent with equilibrium.

This insight, that when effort is endogenous unemployment must be present to motivate workers, is at the heart of modern efficiency wage theory. It provides the rationale for the link between productivity and the wage rate and it generates a model with simultaneous wage rigidity and unemployment. This basic idea has been suggested by a number of authors as a possible explanation for unemployment (see, for example, Calvo 1979; Foster and Wan 1984; Miyazaki 1984; and Shapiro and Stiglitz 1984). All of the models are similar in structure and include the assumption that effort can only be imperfectly monitored by the firm so that it is possible to shirk and not get caught. The wage rate must then rise to a level that generates unemployment high enough to persuade workers that working hard is in their own best interest. In this section I focus on the Shapiro/Stiglitz model, the simplest of those adopting this approach, to demonstrate exactly how these models work.

To keep matters simple, Shapiro and Stiglitz use a one-good model in which infinitely lived employees can either work hard (put out an effort level of $\hat{e}$) or shirk (put out no effort). The price of the consumption good is normalized at 1 and agents are not allowed to save. The utility of a typical worker is equal to the difference between the wage earned (since all income is spent on the consumption good) and the effort expended on the job. That is

(3) $U = w - \hat{e}.$

If the agent is employed and chooses to work hard, then there is an exogenous probability (b) that he will lose his or her job. Such separations are assumed to be caused by firm closings due to relocation and/or shifts in tastes and preferences. If the worker shirks, there is an additional probability (q) of being fired. This represents the probability of being caught shirking. While employed, the worker earns the market-determined wage (w) and while unemployed he or she collects unemployment insurance of $\bar{w}$. Finally, the probability of finding a job (a) is assumed to be a decreasing function of the unemployment rate (μ).

It is optimal for an employed worker to expend effort if the expected lifetime income from doing so exceeds the expected lifetime income from shirking. To determine when this is the case, let V_s^e denote the expected lifetime utility for a worker who is currently employed and shirking and let V_n^e represent the expected lifetime utility for a hard-working employee. Then, if we let r denote the interest rate, it follows that

(4) $V_s^e = \dfrac{w + (b + q)V_u + (1 - b - q)V_s^e}{1 + r}$

and

(5) $V_n^e = \dfrac{w - \hat{e} + bV_u + (1 - b)V_n^e}{1 + r}$

where V_u denotes the expected lifetime utility for an unemployed worker. Intuitively, (4) states that an employed, shirking worker earns a wage of w and expends no effort so that current utility is given by w (applying eq. (3)). Moreover, these workers face a probability of $b + q$ that they will lose their job either because of being caught shirking (which occurs with probability q) or due to an exogenous shock (which occurs with probability b), in which case their expected future income is equal to V_u. If they keep their job (which occurs with probability $1 - b - q$), their expected lifetime income remains equal to V_s^e. The denominator represents the rate at which future income is discounted. Equation (5) can be explained in a similar manner. The only difference is that hard-working employees expend effort so that current utility is lower ($w - \hat{e}$), but they are rewarded for their effort by a smaller probability of unemployment (b).

The expected lifetime income for an unemployed worker is calculated in an analogous fashion. We have

$$(6) \quad V_u = \frac{\bar{w} + a(\mu)V_n^e + (1 - a(\mu))V_u}{1 + r}.$$

The worker collects unemployment insurance of $\bar{w}$ while facing an employment probability of a (which is a decreasing function of μ, the unemployment rate). If a job is found, expected lifetime income rises to V_n^e; otherwise, it remains at V_u.

Employed workers shirk if $V_s^e > V_n^e$ and expend effort if the inequality is reversed. Solving (4) – (6) for V_s^e, V_n^e and V_u allows us to generate the *no shirk condition* (NSC). This condition tells us for any given level of unemployment how high the market wage must be to guarantee that employed workers will not loaf on the job. We find that $V_n^e \geq V_s^e$ if

$$(7) \quad w \geq \bar{w} + \frac{\hat{e}}{q} (a + b + r + q).$$

This condition can be simplified a bit further by noting that in equilibrium the flows into and out of unemployment must be equal. The flow out of unemployment is proportional to $a\mu$, the product of the employment probability and the unemployment rate, while the flow into unemployment is proportional to $b(1 - \mu)$, the product of the separation rate and

the employment rate (assuming no employed workers shirk).[4] Equating
these two rates, solving for a and substituting into (7) yields a somewhat
simplified version of the no shirk condition:

$$(8) \quad w \geq \bar{w} + \hat{e} + \frac{\hat{e}}{q} [\frac{b}{\mu} + r].$$

Equation (8) reveals that the wage firms must pay to induce workers
to expend effort on the job increases with unemployment insurance and
the separation rate. Intuitively, as unemployment compensation rises
there is less of a reason to fear unemployment and workers are more
likely to risk losing their jobs by shirking. In addition, if the separation
rate is relatively high, workers may as well shirk since they are likely
to lose their jobs in the near future anyway.

Equation (8) also indicates that the "no shirk wage" is decreasing
in the probability that shirking will be detected (q) and the unemployment rate. If q is relatively high so that monitoring of effort is fairly
efficient and effective, the firm can pay a low wage without fearing
that its workers will shirk. After all, shirking would be detected easily
and the worker would lose his job. The unemployment rate is a factor,
since it influences the rate at which jobs can be obtained. An increase
in the unemployment rate makes it harder for an unemployed worker
to find a job. Therefore, an employed worker values his job more and
is much less likely to risk losing it by shirking during periods of high
unemployment. This allows the firm to pay a lower wage when μ is high.

The NSC is depicted in figure 5.1 with employment (L) measured
on the horizontal axis and the wage on the vertical axis. For any given
level of employment, wages above the NSC are sufficient to induce effort while wages below the NSC lead workers to shirk. The efficiency
wage, $w(\mu)$, is an increasing function of employment since reductions
in unemployment make it easier to find new jobs and must therefore
be accompanied by higher wages to make working hard optimal. At
full employment (L_f), shirking is optimal regardless of the wage since
workers can find new jobs at the old wage as soon as they are fired.
Therefore, the efficiency wage curve approaches but never intersects
the dashed vertical line. This implies that full employment can never be

an equilibrium. Equilibrium unemployment serves as a discipline device by making workers fear the prospect of losing their jobs.

Figure 5.1

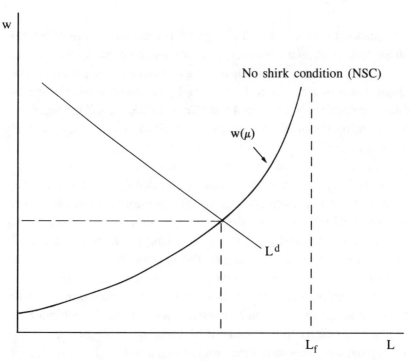

Worker behavior is completely described by the NSC. To complete the model we must also take into account firm behavior. The firm must choose w, the wage it pays to its employed workers; $\bar{w}$, unemployment compensation; and L, employment, taking as given the economy's overall unemployment rate. The optimal wage is given by (8) (with the inequality replaced by an equality), since this is the lowest wage that will elicit effort. Increasing $\bar{w}$ is costly for two reasons: it increases layoff costs and raises the efficiency wage. Thus, it is optimal to set $\bar{w}$ as low as the law allows. Finally, given w and $\bar{w}$, the firm chooses L to maximize profit. This leads to a labor demand schedule which is, as is usually the case, downward sloping. The aggregate demand for labor is represented by the L^d curve in figure 5.1.

Equilibrium occurs at the intersection of the labor demand curve and efficiency wage locus. As emphasized above, equilibrium unemployment must be positive. Changes in effort requirements, the laws governing unemployment compensation, the process by which workers find jobs, the ability of firms to monitor effort, and other such variables influence unemployment and wages by affecting the labor demand schedule and the no shirk condition. For example, an increase in the separation rate (implying greater job turnover) makes it harder for firms to keep workers from shirking. This leads to an increase in w and, as the no shirk condition shifts up, an increase in unemployment as well. The nature of the relationships between some of the remaining factors and unemployment are discussed in some detail in the policy section below.

In chapter 2 we found that in the presence of trading frictions equilibrium unemployment is generally suboptimal. The reason for this is that external effects are generated by individual search decisions and this distorts incentives. It is therefore natural to ask whether the unemployment produced by efficiency wage considerations is efficient. The answer is generally no, for reasons similar to those encountered in the search literature. There are two externalities that arise in the firm's hiring decision that can be explained as follows. An increase in employment by one firm lowers the unemployment rate and makes it easier for an unemployed worker to find a job. This increases the expected lifetime income of the unemployed and raises the efficiency wage that all other firms must pay. This externality remains important even when the number of firms becomes large since, although the effect on unemployment is small, the number of firms affected is large. This negative externality leads to overemployment.

The second externality concerns the difference between the private and social costs of employment. When a firm considers hiring another worker it considers only the private cost, w. However, the social cost of employment is $\hat{e}$, the effort expended by the worker. The no shirk condition (eq. (8)) indicates that in equilibrium $w > \hat{e}$ so that the private cost exceeds the social cost. This leads to underemployment. By combining the two external effects, we can conclude that equilibrium unemployment may be either too high or too low for efficiency purposes. Shapiro and Stiglitz show that in their model the two effects exactly offset each other if, in equilibrium, the marginal and average products of labor are equal. In general, however, this need not be the case.

Further complications arise when the model is extended to allow for an endogenously determined amount of monitoring. This is accomplished by making q a function of the firm's monitoring effort (m) and by subtracting the cost of monitoring from profit (as given in eq. (1)). Since Changes in q affect the efficiency wage (see eq. (8)), changes in monitoring effort will generate externalities similar to those associated with the hiring decision. The implication is that the level of monitoring will, in general, be suboptimal and this will have spillover effects on unemployment. In the Shapiro/Stiglitz framework with a constant returns to scale production function, equilibrium entails too much monitoring and overemployment. Intuitively, firms can reduce shirking by increasing the amount of monitoring that they undertake. However, since monitoring uses resources, it is cheaper for society to reduce shirking through layoffs. With constant returns to scale, the savings in resources more than compensate for the loss in employment, so that it is optimal to tax monitoring. However, this is not true in general.

(ii) Criticisms and Evidence

Efficiency wage theory has been both severely criticized and staunchly defended in recent years. Most of the criticisms have been aimed at demonstrating that there are superior ways of handling the shirking problem that are more likely to emerge in a market setting.[5] For example, it has been argued that each worker should be willing to post a bond that would be forfeited if he or she was detected shirking. All that would be needed to guarantee that the worker would not shirk would be a sufficiently high bond; unemployment would no longer be needed as a discipline device. Alternatively, the worker could pay an "entrance fee" when initially hired. Competition among workers for the jobs would then increase the fee until all involuntary unemployment disappeared.

The fear of losing your job and having to pay another entrance fee would then be sufficient to keep workers from shirking.

The initial response to this criticism was to point out that this type of bonding creates a moral hazard problem for the firm when it monitors its workforce. After all, what prevents the firm from simply claiming that the worker has shirked (regardless of the truth) in order to collect the bond? Or, in the case of entrance fees, why not simply fire the worker in order to collect additional fees from the replacement? There is no cost to doing so, since the worker could be replaced immediately by anyone from the pool of unemployed. Unfortunately, at least for the proponents of efficiency wage theory, there are bonding arrangements that both elicit effort and avoid this moral hazard problem. For example, upon accepting a job, each worker could deposit the value of the bond into a pension fund. In the event that the worker leaves (for whatever reason), the money would then be used to increase the pension benefits of those who stayed on the job. Since the firm would no longer benefit from firing the worker, this would circumvent the moral hazard problem.[6] Supporters tend to argue that such arrangements are rarely observed due to imperfections in capital markets which make it impossible for the newly employed to raise the value of the bond.[7] Further work merging contract and efficiency wage theories is needed to determine if there is a more satisfactory answer to the question of why such contracting arrangements do not emerge to handle the shirking problem.

Support for efficiency wage theory has come from a variety of sources. On the theoretical front, a number of authors, most notably Akerlof and Yellin (1986), argue that efficiency wage theory is able to explain a number of important stylized facts concerning cyclical unemployment better than competing micro theories of unemployment, e.g., search and contract theories. Akerlof and Yellin single out the five following features of business cycles that they feel any reasonable model of unemployment should be able to explain:

(1) equilibrium unemployment should be involuntary;

(2) shifts in aggregate demand should affect output and employment;

(3) quits should fall when unemployment rises;

(4) higher-skilled workers should be unemployed less often than lower-skilled workers; and,

(5) labor productivity should vary procyclically.

The first three features can be explained using the simple models discussed above. Unemployment is involuntary since there are jobless workers willing to work at wages slightly below the equilibrium level who are unable to find employment. Moreover, shifts in aggregate demand alter the demand for labor and trigger changes in output and employment. Finally, as unemployment grows it becomes harder to find a new job so that the value of quitting falls. This leads workers to quit less often.

The fourth feature is somewhat more difficult to explain. At first, one might think that it would be more difficult to monitor high-skilled, highly educated workers since their output is more difficult to observe. Therefore, if unemployment acts as a discipline device and if all workers possess the same utility function, then there should be more unemployment among high-skilled workers. However, Akerlof and Yellin argue that, in reality, high-skilled jobs are more pleasant and cause less disutility when effort is expended. If high-skilled workers gain no utility from shirking, then, in equilibrium there will be no highly skilled workers unemployed. Unemployment will still be necessary to motivate low-skilled workers and the desired result will be obtained.

To explain the remaining feature, a model combining elements of the efficiency wage and contract theories is needed. These considerations enter by assuming that effort can vary and that the wage is negotiated in an uncertain environment before the state of the world is known. In a model without informational asymmetries and work-sharing it can be shown (using techniques outlined in the previous chapter) that an optimal contract is characterized by a wage that is independent of the economic environment and an effort function that varies procyclically. That is, workers work harder during good periods. However, this does not immediately imply that productivity varies procyclically since effort is subject to diminishing returns. Nevertheless, the desired result can be obtained under certain conditions. For more details on this argument, see Akerlof and Yellin (1986, pp. 11-14).

Additional support for the theory is provided by Bulow and Summers (1986), who argue that efficiency wage considerations provide a theoretical basis for the dual labor market hypothesis. This hypothesis maintains that there are two distinct labor markets: one providing high-paying primary sector jobs and another providing low-paying secondary sector jobs.[8] This theory has long been criticized for its lack of theoretical underpinnings. Why don't secondary workers migrate to the primary sector and bid wages down to their market-clearing level? Bulow and Summers argue that shirking and imperfect monitoring provide the explanation. In their model, shirking is difficult to detect in the primary sector and perfect monitoring is costless in the secondary sector. The secondary sector acts as a competitive labor market with wages adjusting to clear the market. Without unemployment, the only way to keep primary sector workers from shirking is to pay them wages above this level. This makes primary sector jobs more attractive than secondary sector jobs and supplies the motivation for primary sector employees to work hard in order to avoid losing their jobs.

On the empirical front, several approaches have been adopted to either test the theory or provide support for it. First, there is some compelling anecdotal evidence that paying higher wages leads to greater productivity, either due to higher morale or less shirking (see, for example, the discussion concerning Ford's 1914 wage increase in Bulow and Summers 1986). In addition, there is evidence that high wages tend to reduce turnover costs (by lowering quit rates), increase job satisfaction (Hamermesh 1977), and reduce absenteeism (Allen 1984).

There have also been a few attempts to determine whether or not inter-industry wage data are consistent with the predictions of the efficiency wage models (e.g., Dickens and Katz 1986; Katz 1986b; Krueger and Summers 1988; and Katz and Summers 1989). As I emphasized in the chapter on search theory, we often observe workers with similar skills and jobs earning substantially different wages. Competitive models of the labor market cannot explain why such differentials persist. According to search theory this phenomenon could arise as the result of search costs that vary across workers. Efficiency wage models provide another possible explanation: these differentials could be due to different wage/productivity relationships across industries. If, for example, monitoring is more difficult in one industry than another, efficiency wage theory would predict higher wages in the difficult to monitor industry. It has been argued that the fact that there are important wage differentials that cannot be explained by standard competitive factors, e.g., compensating differentials, differences in union coverage, labor quality differences, is evidence in favor of this theory (see, for example, Krueger and Summers 1988). Given the wealth of other possible explanations for this phenomenon (including search theory), this must be considered, at best, weak evidence. For a detailed survey of the empirical work along these lines see Katz (1986a). For an appropriately skeptical view of this approach see Topel (1989).

To date, direct attempts to test the theory have proven to be largely unsuccessful (see Leonard 1987; Groshen and Krueger 1990; and Holzer 1990).

(iii) Policy Implications

The policy implications of efficiency wage theory are similar in many respects to those generated by search theory. This is especially true with respect to transfer payments from the government. Unemployment insurance (and other transfers to the unemployed) increase unemployment for two reasons. First, it makes workers less fearful of unemployment by reducing the relative value of a job. In response, firms must pay higher wages in order to keep workers from shirking. This can be seen most clearly in (8), the NSC, where the efficiency wage is an increasing function of $\bar{w}$, unemployment compensation. The second effect works through labor demand. Since firms must finance at least part of the program, any increase in UI raises the cost of employment and lowers labor demand. Therefore, both the NSC and the labor demand curve in figure 5.1 shift in a manner that lowers employment. In an economy with multiple sectors, an increase in UI will shift resources toward the high unemployment/high-wage sectors. The reason for this is that workers become more willing to risk long spells of unemployment in order to have the chance to capture a high-wage job. This result also parallels the effect of UI in a search model.

Transfer payments to employed workers or firms filling vacancies (such as wage or employment subsidies and job bonus programs) increase employment. If the payment is made to labor, it makes employment a more valuable state and shifts the NSC in figure 5.1 down. If the payment goes to the firm, it reduces the relative value of an unfilled vacancy (with respect to a filled vacancy) and shifts labor demand in figure 5.1 out to the right. As with unemployment insurance, the qualitative effect is identical to what is predicted by a search model.

Figure 5.1 can also be used to determine the impact of an increase in the minimum wage. To do so, draw a horizontal line at the level of the minimum wage over to the NSC. This gives the NSC when the law is instituted. In sectors in which the minimum wage falls below the level of the original equilibrium wage, the law has no impact. Otherwise, the new NSC intersects labor demand at a lower level of employment—as we would expect, unemployment rises. Assuming that these low-wage sectors are also the low unemployment sectors (as should be the case according to the theory), the program results in resources shifting towards high unemployment sectors of the economy.

Turn next to the impact of state-run employment agencies which are aimed at reducing the time it takes to find a job. In the Shapiro/Stiglitz model, such a program can be modeled by examining the impact of a reduction in a, the job-finding rate. The immediate impact is a reduction in the time it takes to find reemployment. While this lowers unemployment, it also makes workers fear unemployment less and therefore shifts the NSC up. Although this indirect effect works in the opposite direction of the primary effect, causing unemployment to rise, it can never dominate.

There are two other similarities between the policy implications of the search and efficiency wage literatures worth mentioning. The first concerns trade policy and is due to Bulow and Summers (1986). In their two-sector model they demonstrate that free trade can actually lower welfare if it results in a contraction of the primary (i.e., efficiency wage) sector. The reasoning is as follows. Primary sector jobs carry with them higher wages to keep workers from shirking. If this sector shrinks due to free trade, high wage (i.e., "good jobs") are replaced by low wage ('bad jobs') and income falls. This can result in a fall in welfare. In fact, welfare is likely to fall if the primary sector is highly competitive, since then the standard gains from trade would be relatively small and would probably be dominated by the fall in income. The implication is that governments should subsidize or protect high-wage, highly competitive sectors. This result is similar to Davidson, Martin, and Matusz's finding that some jobs are more valuable than others in an economy with search-generated unemployment and finitely lived agents.

Finally, turn to the question of efficiency. As we noted above, externalities are present in efficiency wage models that render equilibrium suboptimal. There are some cases in which it is necessary to increase unemployment in order to raise welfare. However, as with the search literature, there is no evidence that these externalities are nontrivial nor is there any indication of which external effects are most important. It is therefore impossible to determine the overall welfare effect of any given policy; the results will not be robust to small changes in the assumptions of the model.

C. The Insider/Outsider Theory of Unemployment

The fundamental supposition of the insider/outsider theory of unemployment is that the workforce can be divided into two subgroups that possess different degrees of power in the wage-setting process. The first subgroup consists of employed workers (the "insiders") while the second consists of the unemployed (the "outsiders").[9] It is also assumed that turnover costs or frictions exist that insulate the wages earned by the insiders from market forces. This results in non-Walrasian wages and involuntary unemployment.

The basic idea is simple. A firm has a certain amount of time and effort already invested in its current workforce. It took time to find and train the right workers for each available job. Replacing these workers with outsiders would be costly for a number of reasons. For example, the firm would have to search for and then train the new workers, and it might be costly to lay off or fire the old incumbents. These transaction costs provide the insiders with a certain amount of market power that they can use to their advantage. Insiders can demand wages above the market-clearing level and, as long as their demands do not become too outrageous (so that it becomes cheaper to fire the worker and seek an outsider as a substitute), the firm will find it optimal to meet the demand. In equilibrium, even though outsiders would strictly prefer to be employed, insiders are able to exploit their market power to keep outsiders from underbidding them and taking their jobs. This results in involuntary unemployment.

In the remainder of this chapter I briefly outline how insider market power results in unemployment, and how such market power can be obtained and sustained. Recent empirical tests of the theory's predictions are also discussed.

(i) Bargaining, Non-Walrasian Wages and Involuntary Unemployment

One of the first papers to formally analyze the impact of insider market power is due to Shaked and Sutton (1984). The purpose of their article is to show how trading frictions and turnover costs can lead to non-Walrasian outcomes. They do so by assuming that such costs exist and then demonstrating how insiders can exploit the situation and secure wages above the market-clearing level.

In Shaked and Sutton's model, a firm and its employees bargain over wages by trading offers until one side makes an offer that the other side finds acceptable. However, the firm has the option of terminating negotiations with its current workforce and replacing it with unemployed workers if agreement cannot be reached in T periods. If the firm chooses this option, the newly hired workers become the new insiders and negotiations begin anew. The option of replacing workers captures the notion that market forces should influence the outcome of the negotiations. If, for example, unemployment is high, one might expect that there would be a great deal of competition for the employment opportunities offered by the firm and that this would drive the wage rate down to its market-clearing level. The assumption that this option can be exercised only after T periods have passed captures the notion that there are frictions or turnover costs that keep the firm from *costlessly* replacing its workforce. Increases in T indicate that it takes more time and effort (that is, it is costlier) to replace insiders with outsiders. Large values for T are therefore associated with a high degree of insider market power.

The solution to this complex bargaining problem can be explained in a fairly straightforward, intuitive manner. Following Shaked and Sutton, consider the case in which the firm collects \$1 in revenue and must negotiate with its single employee over the wage. Assume further that the firm, its worker and the outsider discount the future at a common rate denoted by $\delta \epsilon (0,1)$. Finally, assume that this is the only job available so that the competitive solution results in the workers underbidding each other until the wage is driven to zero.

The bargaining problem can be thought of as a two-stage process. In the first stage, which lasts T periods, the firm is bound to negotiate with its current employee. Then, if after T periods no agreement has been reached, we enter stage two in which the firm is free to switch workers or keep bargaining with the incumbent worker. Let M denote the most that the firm can reasonably expect to earn at the beginning of stage one and let M^0 represent the most that the firm can reasonably expect to earn if it reaches the beginning of stage two. Then the following two equations must hold

$$(9) \quad M^0 = \max\{\delta(1 - \delta + \delta M^0); M\}$$

$$(10) \quad M = \frac{1 - \delta^{T+1}}{1 - \delta} + \delta^T M^0.$$

Equation (9) can be explained as follows. Consider the position of the firm if it reaches stage two. At this point, it will either switch workers or continue bargaining with its current employee based on which action leads to the larger payoff. If it switches, it finds itself in a setting identical to that faced at the beginning of stage one; the only difference is that the old insider has been replaced by another worker. Therefore, switching leads to a payoff of M. Now, suppose instead that the firm chooses to continue bargaining with the incumbent worker. If the next two offers (one made by the firm and then the counteroffer made by the insider) are refused, then the firm finds itself in exactly the same position it was in at the start of the negotiations (since it is now locked into bargaining with this worker for at least T more periods). Therefore, in this case, the firm's payoff will be at most $\delta^2 M^0$. Go back one period. The worker, realizing that the firm will give up at least $\delta^2 - \delta^2 M^0$ in the next period, demands at least this value now. This leaves the firm with $\delta - [\delta^2 - \delta^2 M^0]$ or $\delta[1 - \delta + \delta M^0]$, a value that it can demand at the beginning of the negotiations.

Turn next to (10). This equation can be explained by working backwards in a similar manner. If no agreement is reached after T periods, the firm will earn no more than $\delta^T M^0$. Therefore, in period T the firm can expect a profit of no more than $\delta^T - \delta^T M^0$. Repeating this argument T times leads to a profit of no more than

$$1 - \delta - \delta^2 - \ldots - \delta^T + \delta^T M^0 = \frac{1 - \delta^{T+1}}{1 - \delta} + \delta^T M^0$$

at the beginning of the negotiations.

Solving (9) and (10) for the two unknowns, M and M^0, yields the firm's equilibrium profits

(11) $$M = \frac{1 - \delta^{T+1}}{(1 + \delta)(1 - \delta^T)}.$$

Examining (11) in detail reveals that the market-clearing wage, i.e., zero, is obtained only if $T = 1$ and that the wage is increasing in T (since profits are decreasing in T). That is, only when the firm can immediately switch workers (so that there are no turnover costs or frictions) will the wage be bid down to its competitive level. For all other values of T, a non-Walrasian wage rate is obtained. We conclude that frictions or turnover costs produce an environment in which incumbent workers are able to secure wages above the market-clearing level for themselves. They are able to do so because the frictions bestow upon them market power that places them at a relative advantage when compared with the unemployed outsiders. In a more complex model with multiple sectors and firms, this market power would lead to an equilibrium level of involuntary unemployment.

The one shortcoming of the Shaked and Sutton analysis is that it does not attempt to explain why outsiders cannot (or do not) seek out the firms and underbid the insiders. This is because they simply assume that the firm and the outsiders cannot make contact for T periods. We now turn to the model that addresses this issue.

(ii) Turnover Costs and On-the-Job Harassment

In a series of articles, Lindbeck and Snower (1986, 1987, 1988a, 1988b) argue that insiders are able to prevent outsiders from underbidding them by using their market power to alter the transaction costs faced by their employers. For example, suppose that there are significant search and training costs involved in hiring new workers and that firing costs are nontrivial. Then, even if outsiders are willing to work for less than the prevailing wage, they may not be willing to accept work at the prevailing wage less the turnover costs the firm must incur when hiring them. Therefore, insiders will be able to retain their jobs, underbidding will be unsuccessful and unemployment will persist. The higher the turnover costs, the larger the wage rate insiders will be able to earn before underbidding becomes successful. It is therefore in the insiders' interest to increase these costs as much as possible. One way to do so is through unionization, since unions can push for increased severance pay and institute elaborate hiring and firing procedures that make substituting outsiders for insiders extremely costly. In addition, strike threats are more powerful when coming from a group of workers (rather than individuals) and can further enhance the market power of insiders.

Another way that insiders can increase transaction costs is by threatening not to cooperate with and/or to harass newly hired employees. As Lindbeck and Snower demonstrate in their 1988 *AER* article, such threats can keep outsiders from "stealing" jobs held by insiders. In their model, worker productivities depend upon the level of cooperation between workers and the amount of cooperation that takes place is under the control of the workers. In equilibrium, insiders cooperate with other insiders but harass any outsider who takes a job from a fellow insider. This lowers outsider productivity and hence the value of outsiders to the firm. Underbidding would not take place either because outsiders would realize that it would be unsuccessful or because firms would realize that replacing high-productivity insiders with low-productivity outsiders would not be profitable. Since outsiders prefer to trade places with insiders, the unemployment is involuntary. This unemployment arises as the result of insiders exploiting their market power to keep outsiders from obtaining jobs.

(iii) Criticism and Evidence

The insider/outsider theory of unemployment generates several interesting testable hypotheses. One particular result which has received a great deal of attention has to do with the multiplicity of equilibria and the persistence of unemployment. Since insiders possess and use market power to their own advantage, the number of insiders is an important determinant of the equilibrium unemployment rate. Different initial employment levels produce different equilibria; there is no "natural rate of unemployment." Moreover, the effect of different labor market policies will depend, to a large extent, on the initial level of employment. Recent empirical work by Blanchard and Summers (1987) indicates that in fact the equilibrium unemployment rate does depend on the history of the actual employment level. This result has been referred to as "hysteresis in unemployment," since it implies that equilibrium is path-dependent. Insider/outsider theory provides one possible explanation for this empirical finding.

Additional support for this theory can be found in recent work by Carruth and Oswald (1987) and Blanchflower, Oswald and Garrett (1987). These papers attempt to explain how wages are determined in British labor markets. In addition, they focus on the importance of internal and external pressures in the wage-setting process. External pressures are beyond the firm's control and include standard competitive factors such as the level of unemployment. Internal pressures include factors such as the profitability of the firm. According to competitive theories of the labor market it is the outside pressures that should drive wages. However, in both instances inside factors are found to also be of great importance. This is consistent with the insider/outsider theory since internal pressures affect the degree of market power held by insiders.

Due to the relative newness of this theory, it has not yet generated a great deal of attention from those who are apt to criticize it. There are, however, two obvious weaknesses of the models in their present form. First, although the models explain why existing firms will not want to hire outsiders, it seems as if it would be profitable for new firms to enter, hire outsiders at low wages, and compete with the incumbents. As long as the prevailing wage was above the market-clearing level and as long as set-up costs are not too large, it appears that entry would be successful at reducing or eliminating unemployment. Therefore, the insider/outsider theory may not be consistent with long-run equilibrium.

The second weakness concerns the payment scheme for insiders. It is assumed throughout that all workers are paid using simple time-rate wages. Under this assumption, there is no way for the firm to convince insiders to cooperate with newly hired workers. However, if the firm used a more elaborate payment scheme in which insider compensation was tied to firm profitability (or output), it might be in the insiders' interest to allow the firm to expand by hiring outsiders at low pay. By doing so, the firm could increase its profit and insiders would benefit as well. For this reason, "share contracts" would improve the performance of the economy and reduce unemployment (for more on share contracts see Weitzman 1984 and 1987). Although Lindbeck and Snower (1988a) suggest some reasons why such contracts are rarely observed, it is clear that more research along these lines is warranted.

(iv) Policy Implications

The insider/outsider theory of unemployment is still in its infancy, and at this point, therefore, little work has been undertaken to investigate its policy implications. What follows relies heavily on one of the only systematic treatments of policy issues in this framework, chapter 10 of Lindbeck and Snower (1988b).

With respect to labor market policies, Lindbeck and Snower consider two avenues to increase employment: policies that diminish insider power and those that increase the participation of outsiders in the wage-setting process. To reduce insider power it is necessary to find ways to lower the cost of replacing incumbent workers. One way to do this is to lower severance pay or decrease the proportion of the unemployment insurance program funded by firms. Another way is to alter legislation so as to make firing workers easier. According to the theory, such policy changes should result in lower wages for insiders, an increase in employment and greater production. There is a cost, however, in that the real wages of insiders must fall for these policies to be effective.

One method for increasing outsiders' influence in the process of negotiation has already been mentioned: the institution of profit-sharing schemes. By tying worker compensation to firm performance, the cost of hiring new workers falls and incumbent workers become less resistant to expanding employment (this follows from the fact that by expanding employment firms can increase profits; this benefits insiders if they receive part of the firm's profit). The government can encourage the use of such labor contracts via tax incentives.

Another way to make outsiders more attractive to firms is for the government to subsidize training programs. This lowers the cost of hiring outsiders and increases labor productivity at a cost of reducing insider wages. Finally, any government policies aimed at encouraging entry by new firms should increase employment. After all, new firms do not have incumbent workers and are therefore free to hire outsiders at relatively low wages. This can be accomplished by encouraging lending institutions to finance new ventures or by altering the tax incentives faced by firms.

NOTES

1. See also Stiglitz (1976) or Yellin (1984).

2. If the relationship between productivity and the wage varies across firms the model predicts that the firms will offer different wages. Thus, this is perhaps another explanation of equilibrium wage dispersion.

3. Shapiro and Stiglitz were not the first to argue that by paying higher wages firms could elicit greater effort. Examples of earlier work which also exploits this notion include Eaton and White (1982), Foster and Wan (1984) and Miyazaki (1984).

4. The actual flows out of and into unemployment are found by multiplying these values by the size of the labor force. It is also worth noting that in equilibrium firms will pay efficiency wages so that no worker will shirk.

5. For a more basic criticism aimed at the credibility of the theory see Barro (1989).

6. See, for example, Malcolmson (1984).

7. For a way around imperfections in the capital market see Carmichael (1985).

8. For a discussion of the dual labor market hypothesis see Doeringer and Piore (1971).

9. Workers holding jobs in sectors with no turnover costs are also sometimes included in the outsider group. These workers are subject to market forces and earn less than insiders.

6
Conclusion

It is highly likely that the theories discussed in this monograph each provide an accurate explanation of some component of unemployment. For example, unemployment generated by search or efficiency wage considerations seems most consistent with our notion of frictional unemployment (or the "natural rate"). However, deviations from the equilibrium unemployment rate are probably better explained by models of non-Walrasian equilibria. To further our understanding of unemployment, serious empirical work needs to be undertaken. Unfortunately, in spite of the fact that a great deal of empirical work has been devoted to unemployment, to date very little has been done to test these theories or distinguish between them. Such work is important, since it would allow us to determine which theories account for a *significant* amount of unemployment.

While a detailed investigation of the ways to empirically distinguish between the theories would certainly be valuable, it is beyond the scope of this monograph. In addition, given my firm belief in the theory of comparative advantage, it seems appropriate to leave this task to those more qualified. There are, however, two other issues that are worth considering. First, it is important to sort out the critical features of the various models that need to be verified empirically. This entails reexamining the crucial results and the assumptions that generate them. Second, it is possible that much can be learned by looking for similarities across models as well as differences. In particular, if there are policies that would be effective in all of the frameworks discussed, then the likelihood that such a policy would be effective in reality is greatly enhanced. Therefore, I will conclude the monograph by trying to distinguish between predictions and conclusions that are "model bound" and those that seem to emerge in all of the recent theories of involuntary unemployment.

A. Empirical Verification

The first two issues I discuss concern the type of unemployment the theories attempt to explain. Of particular interest is whether the bulk of unemployment is structural or frictional, and whether or not changes in unemployment are primarily due to business cycles or sectoral shocks. Although these questions have been addressed by a variety of authors, I will focus on the most recent findings.

Search theory explains unemployment due to the market's failure to match unemployed workers and firms with vacancies. The models of non-Walrasian equilibria explain unemployment as the result of incompatible desires on the part of firms and workers with respect to economic transactions. This incompatibility leads to job rationing. If virtually all of unemployment is of the former variety, it would be wise to devote a good deal of resources to employment agencies and other programs designed to improve the matching process. In a recent article, Abraham (1983) argues that this is not the case. In her article, Abraham shows that the number of workers seeking employment typically exceeds the number of vacant jobs by a significant margin (according to her estimates, the ratio averaged 5.0 during the late 1970s). Since searchers greatly outnumber the number of jobs available, there must be many sectors in which jobs are rationed. We can conclude that unemployment is more than just a simple matching problem—that is, not all unemployment is frictional. It follows that programs aimed at matching workers may not have a significant impact on aggregate unemployment.

Abraham's results also lend support to the non-Walrasian models of unemployment discussed in chapter 3. Further support for the view that job rationing is important is provided by Laffont (1985) in his survey of empirical work on fixed-price models. Laffont summarizes the results obtained by Bouissou, Laffont and Vuong (1983) and Artus, Laroque and Michel (1982), who used survey data to investigate whether the European unemployment experienced during the 1970s was dominated by classical or Keynesian unemployment. The survey data included responses by firms to questions concerning the constraints they perceived as binding. For example, firms were asked: "If you received more orders, could you produce more with your actual capacities?'' An affirmative answer was viewed as an indication of excess supply in the product market. A negative response was viewed as an indication of excess demand in the product market. Following this procedure, the authors concluded that over 60 percent of the firms surveyed viewed themselves as constrained in a manner consistent with Keynesian unemployment. Less than one-quarter responded in a manner consistent with classical unemployment.

Another important issue concerns the ability of these theories to explain *changes* in unemployment. So far, most of the work in these areas has focused on providing a microeconomic rationale for the *existence* of unemployment. Far less work has been devoted to the issue of how unemployment varies over time. In particular, there have only been a few attempts to demonstrate that the forces at work in these models can generate cyclical behavior consistent with the stylized facts of business cycles (for notable exceptions, see the search theoretic approaches by Howitt and McAfee 1988 or Diamond and Fudenberg 1989). The importance of this issue is underscored by the recent findings of Blanchard and Diamond (1989). They begin their paper by noting that the monthly flows into and out of employment in the United States are commonly quite large (close to seven million workers change employment status each month). They then go on to investigate whether such transitions are caused primarily by: sectoral shocks, which require a reallocation of labor across sectors; cyclical shocks, due to changes in aggregate demand; or labor supply shocks. Using a simple matching model, they demonstrate that each type of shock implies a different type of co-movement of unemployment, vacancies, and labor force participation. Applying this theory to the data, they find that changes in unemployment over the past 30 years have been primarily influenced by cyclical, not sectoral, shocks. This finding, although somewhat controversial (see the comments by Hall and Yellin that follow in Brookings), strongly suggests that more attention needs to be paid to the origin of business cycles and the cyclical component of unemployment. Providing an explanation of the existence of unemployment is not enough.

One feature that arose repeatedly throughout the monograph was the possibility of multiple, Pareto-rankable, steady-state equilibria. In the search literature, this result emerges due to externalities in the search process and a feedback mechanism that makes a joint increase in production by all firms profitable. This type of coordination problem also arose in the non-Walrasian models where it was generated by spillover effects across sectors (an increase in one sector's employment increases the demand for the other sector's product so that a joint increase in employment may be welfare-improving). As discussed in the policy sections, this result, if supported by empirical evidence, has important policy implications. In particular, when the economy can get stuck in an equilibrium that is Pareto-dominated by another (higher employment) equilibrium, the government should play an active role in determining both the overall level of economic activity and individual expectations about the future economic environment. However, these policy prescriptions depend crucially upon the assumptions that the search externalities and/or spillover effects are nontrivial and, in the search literature, that the search technology exhibits increasing returns to scale. Yet, no one has attempted to measure these external effects. Moreover, work on the properties of the search technology is still in its infancy. While it is interesting to note that the outcome is theoretically possible, it seems sensible to require some evidence that these assumptions mimic reality before instituting the implied policies.

One way to get some sort of handle on the size of the search externalities is to build a simple theoretical model and then calibrate it, i.e., derive estimates of the unobservable parameters, using data from previous labor market studies. This enables one to obtain estimates of the actual size of the external effects. Recent work by Davidson and Woodbury (1990), using data from the Illinois Unemployment Insurance Bonus Experiment, suggests that the search externalities may be fairly small. One of the problems with this approach is that, as Diamond and Maskin (1979) point out, the results are extremely sensitive to the assumptions made concerning the search technology (Davidson and Woodbury assume that all job contacts are made by workers and that the underlying search technology is quadratic).

Recent findings with respect to the properties of the search technology are no more encouraging. Estimating a model, using British data, in which increasing returns to scale is a necessary condition for multiple equilibria, Pissarides (1986) finds strong evidence in favor of constant returns to scale. Blanchard and Diamond (1989) obtain similar results using U.S. data, although it is possible to interpret their results as support for mildly increasing returns to scale.

B. Similarities in Policy Implications

Although the five theories surveyed rely on dramatically different arguments to support equilibrium unemployment, there is remarkable consistency in terms of the policy implications. One reason for this is that all of the work in these areas can be viewed as an attempt to establish a solid microeconomic foundation for Keynesian unemployment. Not surprisingly, the policy implications that follow possess a distinct Keynesian flavor.

With respect to transfer payments, except in a few minor instances, unemployment compensation increases unemployment by making joblessness relatively more attractive than it would be in the absence of such a program. When search is required to find employment, unemployment compensation reduces search activity and results in fewer matches between firms and workers. When efficiency wage considerations are important, UI raises the wage that firms must pay to keep workers from shirking and this results in a greater steady-state level of unemployment. Unemployment insurance also increases the turnover costs faced by firms, thereby increasing insider market power. This leads to higher insider wages and lower employment according to the insider/outsider theory of unemployment. Only the fixed-price literature provides support for UI. When unemployment is of the Keynesian variety, UI relaxes the product market constraint faced by firms and increases employment. However, even in this case there are alternative programs that can achieve the same objective.

On the other hand, programs that reward workers for finding jobs or firms for filling vacancies, e.g., wage or job subsidies and bonuses to workers finding reemployment, almost always perform well. By making a job more valuable, these programs increase search effort, reduce the expected reward from shirking and increase aggregate demand. All three effects lead to an increase in steady-state employment. The only cost associated with such schemes appears to be distributional.

Not surprisingly, minimum wage laws do not collect much support from these new theories of unemployment. Although they may be welfare-enhancing due to their impact on the externalities involved in search and monitoring, they almost always lead to an increase in unemployment (often by reallocating labor towards high-unemployment sectors). The only exception is when the economy is troubled by the type of Keynesian unemployment discussed in chapter 3. In that case, minimum wages can increase aggregate demand (if they increase aggregate income) and can thereby reduce unemployment. However, as stressed in chapter 3, there are always better ways to achieve the same objective.

Traditional Keynesian remedies for unemployment such as aggregate demand management (through changes in taxes and government spending) also repeatedly emerged throughout the monograph as effective ways to increase welfare. When prices are incorrect due to, say, monopoly power on the part of firms, the constraints faced by firms in the product market can be relaxed by increasing the demand for commodities. This increases the demand for labor and lowers unemployment. Similar effects are present when search and efficiency wage considerations are important. Aggregate demand management can also play an important role in guiding the economy toward the most preferred equilibrium when multiple equilibria are present. As discussed above, this is one possibility that arises in almost all of the frameworks reviewed here.

Finally, we have also seen that when multiple equilibria exist, agents' expectations about the future trading environment are crucial. Government programs aimed at convincing the public that the future economic outlook is positive should be effective ways of improving economic performance. In this sense, the government should act as an "economic cheerleader.'' In other words, the Reagan rhetoric, while not always believable, may have had a hand in reducing unemployment. At least such a belief is consistent with these new views of involuntary unemployment.

References

Abraham, K. 1983. "Structural/Frictional vs. Deficient Demand Unemployment." *American Economic Review* 73(4):708-724.

Akerlof, G. and J. Yellin. 1986. *Efficiency Wage Models of the Labor Market.* New York: Cambridge University Press.

Albrecht, J. and B. Axell. 1984. "An Equilibrium Model of Search Generated Unemployment." *Journal of Political Economy* 92(5):824-40.

Allen, S. 1984. "Trade Unions, Absenteeism and Exit-Voice." *Industrial and Labor Relations Review* 37:331-45.

Arnott, R., A. Hosios, and J. Stiglitz. 1988. "Implicit Contracts, Labor Mobility, and Unemployment." *American Economic Review* 78:1046-1066.

Arrow, K. and G. Debreu. 1954. "Existence of an Equilibrium for a Competitive Economy." *Econometrica* 22:265-290.

Artus, P., G. Laroque, and P. Michel. 1982. "Estimation d'un Modele Macro-Economique Trimestriel Avec Rationnements." Working Paper, INSEE, Paris.

Azariadis, C. 1975. "Implicit Contracts and Underemployment Equilibria." *Journal of Political Economy* 83:1183-1202.

_____. 1978. "Escalator Clauses and the Allocation of Cyclical Risks." *Journal of Economic Theory* 18:119-155.

_____. 1981. "Implicit Contracts and Related Topics: A Survey." In *The Economics of the Labour Market,* ed. Z. Hornstein, et al. London: HMSO.

_____. 1983. "Employment with Asymmetric Information." *Quarterly Journal of Economics* (Supplement) 98:157-172.

Bailey, M. 1974. "Wages and Employment Under Uncertain Demand." *Review of Economic Studies* 41:37-50.

Barro, R. 1989. "An Efficiency Wage Theory of the Weather." *Journal of Political Economy* 97:999-1001.

Barro, R. and H. Grossman. 1971. "A General Disequilibrium Model of Income and Employment." *American Economic Review* 61:82-93.

_____. 1976. *Money, Employment, and Inflation.* New York: Cambridge University Press.

Barron, J. 1975. "Search in the Labor Market and the Durations of Unemployment." *American Economic Review* 65:934-42.

Benassy, J. 1975. "Neo-Keynesian Disequilibrium in a Monetary Economy." *Review of Economic Studies* 42:502-523.

_____. 1976. "The Disequilibrium Approach to Monopolistic Price Setting and General Monopolistic Equilibrium." *Review of Economic Studies* 43:69-81.

_____. 1982. *The Economics of Market Disequilibrium.* New York: Academia Press.

Benhabib, J. and C. Bull. 1983. "Job Search: The Choice of Intensity." *Journal of Political Economy* 91(5): 747-64.

Blanchard, O. and P. Diamond. 1989. "The Beveridge Curve." *Brookings Papers on Economic Activity* 1989(1):1-60.

158

Blanchard, O. and L. Summers. 1987. "Hysteresis in Unemployment." *European Economic Review* 31:288-95.

Blanchflower, D., A. Oswald, and M. Garrett. 1987. "Insider Power in Wage Determination: Part II." Working Paper, London School of Economics.

Bouissou, M., J. Laffont, and Q. Vuong. 1983. "Econometrie du Desequilibre Sur Donnes Microeconomiques." GREMAQ Discussion Paper No. 83, University of Toulouse.

Bowles, S. 1985. "The Production Process in a Competitive Economy." *American Economic Review* 75(1):16-36.

Brechling, F. 1981. "Layoffs and Unemployment Insurance." In *Studies in Labor Markets*, ed. S. Rosen. Chicago: University of Chicago Press.

Brown, C., C. Gilroy, and A. Kohen. 1982. "The Effect of the Minimum Wage on Employment and Unemployment." *The Journal of Economic Literature* 20(2):487-528.

Bull, C. 1987. "The Existence of Self-Enforcing Implicit Contracts." *Quarterly Journal of Economics* 102(1):147-159.

Bulow, J. and L. Summers. 1986. "A Theory of Dual Labor Markets with Applications to Industrial Policy, Discrimination and Keynesian Unemployment." *Journal of Labor Economics* 4:377-414.

Burdett, K. 1978. "Employee Search and Quits." *American Economic Review* 68:212-20.

Burdett, K. and K. Judd. 1983. "Equilibrium Price Dispersion." *Econometrica* 51:955-70.

Calvo, G. 1979. "Quasi-Walrasian Theories of Unemployment." *American Economic Review Proceedings* 69:102-7.

Carmichael, L. 1984. "Reputations in the Labor Market." *American Economic Review* 74:713-725.

————. 1985. "Can Unemployment Be Involuntary?: Comment." *American Economic Review* 75:1213-14.

Carruth, A. and A. Oswald. 1987. "Wage Inflexibility in Britain." *Oxford Bulletin of Economics and Statistics* 49:59-78.

Chari, V. 1983. "Involuntary Unemployment and Implicit Contracts." *Quarterly Journal of Economics* (Supplement) 98:107-122.

Clower, R. 1965. "The Keynesian Counterrevolution: A Theoretical Appraisal." In *The Theory of Interest Rates*, eds. F. Hahn and F. Brechling. London: Macmillan Press.

Cooper, R. 1985. "Worker Asymmetric Information and Employment Distortions." *Journal of Labor Economics* 3:188-208.

————. 1987. *Wage and Employment Patterns in Labor Contracts: Microfoundations and Macroeconomic Implications*. London: Harwood Academic Publishers.

————. 1988. "Optimal Labor Contracts and the Role of Monetary Policy in an Overlapping Generations Model." *Journal of Economic Theory* 44:231-250.

Cooper, R. and A. John. 1988. "Coordinating Coordination Failures in Keynesian Models." *Quarterly Journal of Economics* 103(3): 441-464.

Davidson, C., L. Martin, and S. Matusz. 1987a. "Search, Unemployment, and the Production of Jobs." *Economic Journal* 97:857-76.

_____. 1987b. "Optimal Labor Market Policies with Search Unemployment." Working Paper No. 8706, Michigan State University.

_____. 1988. "The Structure of Simple General Equilibrium Models with Frictional Unemployment." *Journal of Political Economy* 96(6):1267-1293.

_____. 1989. "Dynamic Welfare and the Value of Employment in a Model of Search with Finite Life." Unpublished manuscript.

_____. 1990. "A Search-Theoretic Approach to Unemployment and International Trade: Where Have All the Good Jobs Gone?" Working Paper, Michigan State University.

Davidson, C. and S. Woodbury. 1990. "The Displacement Effect of Reemployment Bonus Programs." Working Paper, Michigan State University.

Diamond, P. 1971. "A Model of Price Adjustment." *Journal of Economic Theory* 3:156-68.

_____. 1981. "Mobility Costs, Frictional Unemployment, and Efficiency." *Journal of Political Economy* 89:798-812.

_____. 1982a. "Aggregate Demand Management in Search Equilibrium." *Journal of Political Economy* 90:881-94.

_____. 1982b. "Wage Determination and Efficiency in Search Equilibrium." *Review of Economic Studies* 49:217-28.

_____. 1984a. "Money in Search Equilibrium." *Econometrica* 52:1-20.

_____. 1984b. *A Search Equilibrium Approach to the Microfoundations of Macroeconomics*. Cambridge: MIT Press.

Diamond, P. and D. Fudenberg. 1989. "Rational Expectations Business Cycles in Search Equilibrium." *Journal of Political Economy* 97(3): 606-619.

Diamond, P. and E. Maskin. 1979. "An Equilibrium Analysis of Search and Breach of Contract I: Steady States." *Bell Journal of Economics* 10(1):282-316.

Dickens, W. and L. Katz. 1986. "Industry Wage Patterns and Theories of Wage Determination." Working Paper, University of California at Berkeley.

Dixit, A. and V. Norman. 1980. *Theory of International Trade*. Cambridge: Cambridge University Press.

Doeringer, P. and M. Piore. 1971. *Internal Labor Markets and Manpower Analysis*. Lexington, MA: D. C. Heath.

Drazen, A. 1980. "Recent Developments in Macroeconomic Disequilibrium Theory." *Econometrica* 48(2):283-306.

Drèze, J. 1975. "Existence of an Equilibrium Under Price Rigidity and Quantity Rationing." *International Economic Review* 16:301-320.

Eaton, B. and W. White. 1982. "Agent Compensation and the Limits of Bonding." *Economic Inquiry* 20:330-43.

Eden, B. 1981. "Toward a Theory of Competitive Price Adjustment." *Review of Economic Studies* 48:199-216.

Evans, A. 1977. "Notes on the Changing Relationship Between Registered Unemployment and Notified Vacancies: 1961-1966 and 1966-1971." *Economica* 44:179-96.

Feldstein, M. 1973. "The Economics of the New Unemployment." *The Public Interest* 33:3-42.

_____. 1975. "The Importance of Temporary Layoffs: An Empirical Analysis." *Brookings Papers on Economic Activity* 3:725-744.

Feldstein, M. and J. Poterba. 1984. "Unemployment Insurance and Reservation Wages." *Journal of Public Economics* 23(1/2):141-67.

Fischer, S. 1977. "Long-Term Contracts, Rational Expectations and the Optimal Money Supply Rule." *Journal of Political Economy* 85:191-205.

Fisher, F. 1972. "On Price Adjustment Without an Auctioneer." *Review of Economic Studies* 39:1-16.

Foster, J. and H. Wan. 1984. "Involuntary Unemployment as a Principal-Agent Equilibrium." *American Economic Review* 74:476-84.

Gal, S., M. Landsberger, and B. Levykson. 1981. "A Compound Strategy for Search in the Labor Market." *International Economic Review* 22(3):597-608.

Gertler, M. 1982. "Imperfect Information and Wage Inertia in the Business Cycle." *Journal of Political Economy* 90:967-987.

Gray, J. 1976. "Wage Indexation: A Macroeconomic Approach." *Journal of Monetary Economics* 2:221-235.

Green, J. and C. Kahn. 1983. "Wage Employment Contracts." *Quarterly Journal of Economics* (Supplement) 98:173-188.

Groshen, E. and A. Krueger. 1990. "The Structure of Supervision and Pay in Hospitals." *Industrial and Labor Relations Review* 43(3):134S-146S.

Grossman, S. and O. Hart. 1981. "Implicit Contracts, Moral Hazard and Unemployment." *American Economic Review* 71:301-308.

_____. 1983. "Implicit Contracts Under Asymmetric Information." *Quarterly Journal of Economics* (Supplement) 98:123-156.

Hahn, F. 1977a. "Exercises in Conjectural Equilibria." *Scandinavian Journal of Economics* 79:210-226.

_____. 1977b. "Unsatisfactory Equilibria." IMSSS Technical Report No. 247, Stanford University.

_____. 1978. "On Non-Walrasian Equilibria." *Review of Economic Studies* 45:1-17.

Hall, R. 1982. "The Importance of Lifetime Jobs in the U.S. Economy." *American Economic Review* 72:716-724.

Hall, R. and D. Lilien. 1979. "Efficient Wage Bargains Under Uncertain Supply and Demand." *American Economic Review* 69:868-879.

Hamermesh, D. 1977. "Economic Aspects of Job Satisfaction." In *Essays in Labor Market Analysis* , eds. O. Ashenfelter and W. Oates. New York: Halstead.

_____. 1987. "What Do We Know About Worker Displacement in the U.S.?" NBER Working Paper No. 2402.

Hart, O. 1982. "A Model of Imperfect Competition With Keynesian Features." *Quarterly Journal of Economics* 97:109-138.

_____. 1983. "Optimal Labour Contracts Under Asymmetric Information: An Introduction." *Review of Economic Studies* 50:3-35.

Heckman, J. and G. Borjas. 1980. "Does Unemployment Cause Future Unemployment? Definitions, Questions and Answers From a Continuous Time Model of Heterogeneity and State Dependence." *Economica* 47:247-83.

Heckman, J. and B. Singer. 1982. "The Identification Problem in Econometric Models for Duration Data." In *Advances in Econometrics,* ed. W. Hildenbrand. Cambridge: Cambridge University Press.

Heller, W. 1986. "Coordination Failure Under Complete Markets With Applications to Effective Demand." In *Equilibrium Analysis: Essays in Honor of Kenneth J. Arrow,* Vol. II, eds. W. Heller, R. Starr, and D. Starrett. Cambridge: Cambridge University Press.

Holmstrom, B. 1983. "Equilibrium Long-Term Contracts." *Quarterly Journal of Economics* (Supplement), 98:23-54.

Holzer, H. 1986. "Reservation Wages and Their Labor Market Effects for White and Black Male Youth." *Journal of Human Resources* 21.

_____. 1987. "Job Search by Employed and Unemployed Youth." *Industrial and Labor Relations Review* 40:601-11.

_____. 1988. "Search Method Use by Unemployed Youth." *Journal of Labor Economics* 6(1):1-20.

_____. 1990. "Wages, Employer Costs and Employee Performance in the Firm." *Industrial and Labor Relations Review* 43(3):147S-164S.

Hosios, A. 1986. "Layoffs, Recruitment and Interfirm Mobility." *Journal of Labor Economics* 4:473-502.

_____. 1990. "On the Efficiency of Matching and Related Models of Search and Unemployment." *Review of Economic Studies* 57(2):279-298.

Howitt, P. and R. McAfee. 1988. "Animal Spirits." Working Paper, University of Western Ontario.

Ioannides, Y. and C. Pissarides. 1983. "Wages and Employment with Firm-Specific Seniority." *Bell Journal of Economics* 14:573-581.

Johnson, W. 1978. "A Theory of Job Shopping." *Quarterly Journal of Economics* 92:261-77.

Jovanovic, B. 1979. "Job-Matching and the Theory of Turnover." *Journal of Political Economy* 87:972-90.

_____. 1983. "Turnover Unemployment and the Cycle." Working Paper, New York University.

_____. 1984. "Matching, Turnover and Unemployment." *Journal of Political Economy* 92:108-22.

Kahn, C. 1985. "Optimal Severance Pay With Incomplete Information." *Journal of Political Economy* 93:435-451.

Katz, L. 1986a. "Efficiency Wage Theories: A Partial Evaluation." In *NBER Macroeconomics Annual 1986,* ed. S. Fischer. Cambridge: MIT Press.

_____. 1986b. "Inter-Industry Wage Structure in Historical Perspective." Working Paper, University of California at Berkeley.

_____. 1986c. "Layoffs, Uncertain Recall and the Duration of Unemployment." NBER Working Paper No. 1825.

162

Katz, L. and L. Summers. 1989. "Industry Rents: Evidence and Implications." In *NBER Microeconomics Annual 1989.* Cambridge: MIT Press.

Kiyotaki, N. 1985. "Implications of Multiple Expectations Equilibria Under Monopolistic Competition." Working Paper, Harvard University.

Krueger, A. and L. Summers. 1988. "Efficiency Wages and the Inter-Industry Wage Structure." *Econometrica* 56:259-94.

Laffont, J. 1985. "Fix Price Models: A Survey of Recent Empirical Work." In *Frontiers of Economics,* eds. K. Arrow and S. Honkapohja. Oxford: Basil Blackwell.

Leibenstein, H. 1957. "The Theory of Underemployment in Densely Populated Backward Areas." In *Economic Backwardness and Economic Growth.* New York: Wiley.

Leijonhufvud, A. 1968. *On Keynesian Economics and the Economics of Keynes.* London: Oxford University Press.

Leonard, J. 1987. "Carrots and Sticks: The Effect of Turnover and Supervisory Effort on Employee Wages." *Journal of Labor Economics* 5:450-87.

Lilien, D. 1980. "The Cyclical Pattern of Temporary Layoffs in United States Manufacturing." *Review of Economics and Statistics* 62:24-31.

Lilien, D. and R. Hall. 1986. "Cyclical Fluctuations in the Labor Market." Chapter 17 in *The Handbook of Labor Economics,* Vol. II, eds. O. Ashenfelter and R. Layard. Amsterdam: North-Holland.

Lindbeck, A. and D. Snower. 1986. "Wage Setting, Unemployment, and Insider/Outsider Relations." *American Economic Review* 76:235-39.

_____. 1987. "Efficiency Wages Versus Insiders and Outsiders." *European Economic Review* 31:407-16.

_____. 1988a. "Cooperation, Harassment, and Involuntary Unemployment: An Insider/Outsider Approach." *American Economic Review* 78:167-88.

_____. 1988b. *The Insider/Outsider Theory of Employment and Unemployment.* Cambridge: MIT Press.

Malcolmson, J. 1984. "Work Incentives, Hierarchy and Internal Labor Markets." *Journal of Political Economy* 92:486-507.

Malinvaud, E. 1977. *The Theory of Unemployment Reconsidered.* Oxford: Basil Blackwell.

Mattila, J. 1974. "Job Quitting and Frictional Unemployment." *American Economic Review* 64:235-39.

McCall, J. 1965. "The Economics of Information and Optimal Stopping Rules." *Journal of Business* 38:300-17.

Mincer, J. and B. Jovanovic. 1981. "Labor Mobility and Wages." In *Studies in Labor Markets,* ed. S. Rosen. Chicago: University of Chicago Press.

Miyazaki, H. 1984. "Work Norms and Involuntary Unemployment." *Quarterly Journal of Economics* 99:297-311.

Moore, J. 1985. "Optimal Labour Contracts When Workers Have a Variety of Privately Observed Reservation Wages." *Review of Economic Studies* 52:37-67.

Morgan, P. 1983. "Search and Optimal Sample Sizes." *Review of Economic Studies* 50:659-75.

Morgan, P. and R. Manning. 1985. "Optimal Search." *Econometrica* 53(4):923-44.

Mortensen, D. 1970. "Job Search, the Duration of Unemployment, and the Phillips Curve." *American Economic Review* 60:505-17.

_____. 1982a. "Property Rights and Efficiency in Mating, Racing and Related Games." *American Economic Review* 72:968-79.

_____. 1982b. "The Matching Process as a Noncooperative Bargaining Game." In *The Economics of Information and Uncertainty*, ed. J. McCall. Chicago: University of Chicago Press.

_____. 1983. "A Welfare Analysis of Unemployment Insurance: Variation on Second Best Themes." *Carnegie-Rochester Series on Public Policy* 19:67-98.

_____. 1986. "Job Search." Chapter 15 in *The Handbook of Labor Economics*, Vol. II, eds. O. Ashenfelter and R. Layard. Amsterdam: North-Holland.

Neary, P. and J. Stiglitz. 1983. "Towards a Reconstruction of Keynesian Economics: Expectations and Constrained Equilibria." *Quarterly Journal of Economics*, (Supplement) 98:199-228.

Obst, N. 1978. "Stabilization Policy with an Inflation Adjustment Mechanism." *Quarterly Journal of Economics* 92(2):355-359.

Parkin, Michael. 1984. *Macroeconomics*. Englewood Cliffs, NJ: Prentice-Hall.

Patinkin, D. 1956. *Money, Interest and Prices*. New York: Row, Peterson and Co.

Pissarides, C. 1979. "Job Matchings With State Employment Agencies and Random Search." *Economic Journal* 89:818-33.

_____. 1984a. "Efficient Job Rejection." *Economic Journal* (Supplement) 94:97-108.

_____. 1984b. "Search Intensity, Job Advertising, and Efficiency." *Journal of Labor Economics* 2:128-43.

_____. 1985. "Taxes, Subsidies and Equilibrium Unemployment." *Review of Economic Studies* 52(1):121-35.

_____. 1986. "Unemployment and Vacancies in Britain." *Economic Policy* 3:499-560.

_____. 1988. "The Search Equilibrium Approach to Fluctuations in Employment." *American Economic Review* 78(2):363-368.

Polemarchakis, H. and L. Weiss. 1978. "Fixed Wages, Layoffs, Unemployment Compensation and Welfare." *American Economic Review* 68:909-917.

Quandt, R. 1978. "Tests of the Equilibrium vs. Disequilibrium Hypothesis." *International Economic Review* 19:435-452.

Quandt, R. and H. Rosen. 1988. *The Conflict Between Equilibrium and Disequilibrium Theories: The Case of the U.S. Labor Market*. Kalamazoo, MI: W.E. Upjohn Institute for Employment Research.

Randolph, W. 1983. *Employment Relationships: Till Death Do Us Part?* Unpublished Ph.D. dissertation, SUNY-Stony Brook.

Reinganum, J. 1979. "A Simple Model of Equilibrium Price Dispersion." *Journal of Political Economy* 87:851-58.

Roberts, J. 1987. "An Equilibrium Model With Involuntary Unemployment at Flexible, Competitive Prices and Wages." *American Economic Review* 77(5):856-874.

Roberts, J. and H. Sonnenschein. 1976. "On the Existence of Cournot Equilibrium Without Concave Profit Functions." *Journal of Economic Theory* 13:112-117.

_____. 1977. "On the Foundations of the Theory of Monopolistic Competition." *Econometrica* 45:101-114.

Rosen, S. 1985. "Implicit Contracts: A Survey." *Journal of Economic Literature* 23:1144-1175.

Rosenfeld, C. 1977. "Job Search of the Unemployed, May 1976." *Monthly Labor Review* 100(11):39-43.

Rothschild, M. 1973. "Models of Market Organization With Imperfect Information: A Survey." *Journal of Political Economy* 81:1283-1308.

_____. 1974. "Searching for the Lowest Price When the Distribution of Prices is Unknown." *Journal of Political Economy* 82:689-711.

Salant, S. 1977. "Search Theory and Duration Data: A Theory of Sorts." *Quarterly Journal of Economics* 91:39-58.

Samuelson, P. 1947. *Foundations of Economic Analysis.* Cambridge: Harvard University Press.

Shaked, S. and J. Sutton. 1984. "Involuntary Unemployment as a Perfect Equilibrium in a Bargaining Model." *Econometrica* 52:1351-64.

Shapiro, C. and J. Stiglitz. 1984. "Equilibrium Unemployment as a Worker Discipline Device." *American Economic Review* 74:433-44.

Solow, R. 1979. "Another Possible Source of Wage Stickiness." *Journal of Macroeconomics* 1:79-82.

_____. 1980. "On Theories of Unemployment." *American Economic Review* 70:1-10.

Stigler, G. 1961. "The Economics of Information." *Journal of Political Economy* 69:213-25.

_____. 1962. "Information in the Labor Market." *Journal of Political Economy* 70:94-104.

Stiglitz, J. 1976. "The Efficiency Wage Hypothesis, Surplus Labor, and the Distribution of Income in L.D.C.s." *Oxford Economic Papers,* 28:185-207.

_____. 1986. "Theories of Wage Rigidity." In *Keynes Economic Legacy: Contemporary Economic Theories,* ed. J. Butkiewicz, et al. New York: Praeger.

Taylor, J. 1980. "Aggregate Dynamics and Staggered Contracts." *Journal of Political Economy* 88:1-23.

Topel, R. 1983. "On Layoffs and Unemployment Insurance." *American Economic Review* 73:541-59.

_____. 1984. "Experience Rating of Unemployment Insurance and the Incidence of Unemployment." *Journal of Law and Economics* 27:61-90.

_____. 1989. "Comment on 'Industry Rents: Evidence and Implications' by L. Katz and L. Summers." In *NBER Microeconomics Annual 1989.* Cambridge: MIT Press.

Viscusi, W. 1979. "Job Hazards and Worker Quit Rates: An Analysis of Adaptive Worker Behavior." *International Economic Review* 20:20-58.

Weitzman, M. 1982. "Increasing Returns and the Foundations of Unemployment Theory." *Economic Journal* 92:787-804.

_____. 1984. *The Share Economy.* Cambridge: Harvard University Press.

_____. 1987. "Steady State Unemployment Under Profit Sharing." *Economic Journal* 97:86-105.

Wilde, L. 1979. "An Information-Theoretic Approach to Job Quits." In *Studies in the Economics of Search,* eds. S. Lippman and J. McCall. New York: North-Holland.

Wright, R. and J. Loberg. 1987. "Unemployment Insurance, Taxes, and Unemployment." *Canadian Journal of Economics* 20(1):36-54.

Woodbury, S. and R. Spiegelman. 1987. "Bonus to Workers and Employers to Reduce Unemployment: Randomized Trials in Illinois." *American Economic Review* 77:513-30.

Yellin, J. 1984. "Efficiency Wage Models of Unemployment." *American Economic Review Proceedings* 74:200-5.

INDEX

Abraham, K., 150
Aggregate demand management policy, 52-54
Akerlof, G., 128, 135, 136
Albrecht, J., 24-25, 49
Allen, S., 137
Arnott, R., 121
Arrow, K., 60
Artus, P., 93n12, 150
Axell, B., 24-25, 49
Azariadis, C., 95, 103, 107, 122, 123nn2, 5

Bailey, M. J., 95, 103
Barro, R. J., 3, 60, 82, 93nn4, 9, 148n5
Barron, J., 56n13
Benassy, J., 3, 80, 84, 93nn4, 7
Benhabib, J., 17-18, 28
Blanchard, O., 145, 151, 153
Blanchflower, D., 145
Bonus payment, 17, 154
Borjas, G., 20
Bouissou, M., 93n12, 150
Bowles, S., 127
Brechling, F., 57n28
Brown, C., 1
Bull, C., 17-18, 28, 119
Bulow, J., 137, 139
Burdett, K., 18, 28
Business cycles, 39-45, 48

Calvo, G., 128
Carmichael, L., 119, 148n7
Carruth, A., 145
Clower, R., 60
Congestion externality: in job search, 33-35; in trade friction analysis, 33-38
Cooper, R., 89, 92, 107, 109, 118, 121, 122, 123n2, 124n6
Coordination failure, 88

Davidson, C., 34, 45, 50, 52, 54-55, 152
Debreu, G., 60
Diamond, P., 3-5, 22, 31, 39, 56nn18, 20, 151, 153
Diamond model, 39-45
Dickens, W., 137
Disequilibrium models. See Non-Walrasian equilibrium
Displaced workers, 30-31
Dixit, A., 83